Passenger Cars 1863-1904

Cars of the World in Colour

PASSENGER CARS
1863-1904

by
T. R. NICHOLSON

Illustrated by
JOHN W. WOOD
Michael Baber
Norman Dinnage
William Hobson
Alan Holliday
Tony Mitchell
Allen Randall

LONDON
BLANDFORD PRESS

ACKNOWLEDGMENTS

The author and the publishers are grateful to the following, who kindly read proofs, suggested alterations, and provided data and references:

From Great Britain:
E. A. Bellamy of Montagu Motor Museum; Anthony Bird; J. R. Davy; D. C. Field; G. N. Georgano; Michael Sedgwick; R. Ivor Slater; C. R. Southall; Veteran Car Club of Great Britain; E. White.

From the United States of America:
Henry Ford Museum, Dearborn, Michigan; W. Everett Miller; Dr. Alfred S. Lewerenz.

From France:
Henri Malartre.

From Italy:
Giancarlo Amari of the Museo dell'Automobile, Turin; Angelo Tito Anselmi; Egon Hanus; Amedeo de Michelis.

From Norway:
Oluf Berrum.

From Sweden:
Scania-Vabis AB.

Printed in Great Britain by
Richard Clay (The Chaucer Press) Ltd, Bungay, Suffolk

INTRODUCTION

The automobile today is part of the furniture. We take it for granted as we do our other chattels. It is more, in fact —it is indispensable, in the way that a bath is more necessary to most people than a television set. At the same time, curiously, it remains intensely desirable, although being available. It is more still —it is thought by some to embody not only our material ambitions, but also our subconscious aspirations, no matter how improbable.

What would we do without it? No other material possession in history has acquired such a concentration of attributes. Yet nobody could say that the automobile was an historical necessity that had to appear. Forty years ago, when men who are only in late middle age now were already adult, it was still a luxury everywhere except in the U.S.A. Sixty years ago, it was regarded as a toy for wealthy eccentrics. Eighty years ago, still within some men's lifetimes, the first tentative vehicles had barely crawled from their handful of little back-street workshops in Europe and America. This book tries, within its compass, to show how it evolved from its earliest beginnings to the end of its first period of development, by which time its main lines were established and it had clearly come to stay.

First, a definition is needed. For present purposes, a 'passenger car' means a working self-propelled vehicle, intended primarily for private, personal transportation, for pleasure as well as necessity. Motor-cycles, buses, trucks, military vehicles and the like are therefore excluded. Thus we also exclude the most famous precursor, Nicolas

Cugnot's first steam-propelled artillery tractor of 1769, and the whole rich and sophisticated flowering of steam coaches, buses, drags, and road trains, developed mainly as public service vehicles in Britain and Europe from the 1820s to the 1840s by Hancock, Gurney, Dance, Dietz, and the rest. We must exclude, too, the first attempts to produce a passenger car as defined that resulted in machines such as Britain's Rickett steamers of 1858–60, which were really scaled-down railroad locomotives. The passenger car had to be light, small, and handy, as well as strong, reliable, and reasonably fast. Therein lay the difficulty. The source of motive power and its fuel had to be portable, compact, and light, yet produce a sufficiency of power.

Little is known about the American Sylvester H. Roper, except that he seems to have been the first man to have produced the earliest solution to the problem that worked, and was more than a flash in the pan. That is, his steam buggies and velocipedes ran consistently enough to be in regular demand at fairs and circuses (as curiosities only, be it noted, as far as the public was concerned), and he persisted, building more than a dozen machines of different types in all, many of them at a time when he had no exact parallels anywhere in the world (1). The French engineers Bouton and Trépardoux, with the vision and backing of the wealthy Comte de Dion (3), soon followed by their compatriot Léon Serpollet, supported by the industrialist Armand Peugeot (7), took the process a stage further in that they were the first

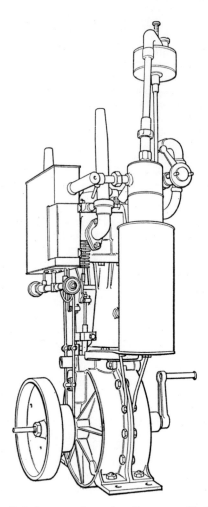

Fig. 1. Daimler vee-twin engine, Germany, 1889 (see 4)

men known to have devised efficient lightweight generators suitable for passenger-car work, and in that their intention was to build cars for sale to the public.

However, by 1883, when De Dion's first light steamer took the road, the motive power that was to displace the established steam engine, by reason of its greater simplicity and ease of starting, was already on the verge of becoming a practical proposition. The Frenchman Lenoir's gas engine, using power tapped from ordinary gas-mains, had been perfected by 1860. It was only suitable for stationary work, but in essence, a light, compact power-pack was there in this first practical internal-combustion engine. Only its fuel rendered it unusable as a propellant for a vehicle. Within twenty-five years the problem had been solved, given Lenoir's initial 'push'. Gasoline, a portable fuel, was the answer. In those early days of the oil industry, gasoline was a mere by-product; the element of petroleum that was distilled off at a lower temperature than paraffin oil (kerosene), which was then the most valuable product. Gasoline, little regarded, was largely wasted. But the experimenters found that it was highly combustible, and volatile enough to make an explosive mixture with air in a carburettor. It was also cheap and plentiful. Markus is said to have built a primitive self-propelled vehicle with a gasoline engine as early as 1864, and the Markus car which survives is attributed to 1875 or 1877 (2). Prompted by Lenoir's engine, the German firm of Otto & Langen in 1876 started to make stationary gas engines on the four-stroke principle set forth by the Frenchman Beau de Rochas in 1862; though Lenoir's were the first gas engines to be a commercial success. The Otto & Langen gas engines were designed by Gottlieb Daimler, who in 1883 made his first gasoline-powered engine. He was interested in its application to various types of land, sea, and air transportation, and in 1886 installed it in a road carriage (4). Karl Benz, another German, was also

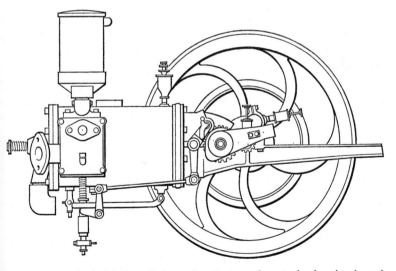

Fig. 2. Benz horizontal single-cylinder engine, Germany, late 1890's, elevation (see 40)

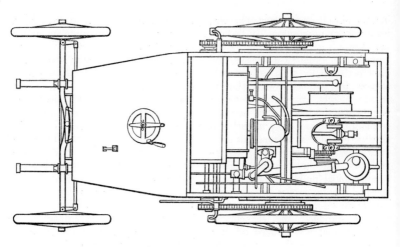

Fig. 3. Benz Velo, Germany, about 1900, plan (see 40)

inspired by the Lenoir engine to manufacture his own stationary gas engines, initially on the two-stroke principle to avoid infringing Otto's patent. Wanting to build a road carriage, while concerned, too, with other forms of self-propelled transportation, his first car was on the road in 1886 (6). Hans Urban Johansen of Denmark, who created the Hammel car, attributed to 1886 (5), had also been in contact with Otto engines. Charles Edgar Duryea, an American, built a gasoline engine in the same year, and his first car seven years later (8). Enrico Bernardi of Italy made his first gasoline engine in 1883, his car following in 1894 (11).

The major basic difference between the first vehicles of Roper, Markus, Daimler, Johansen, and Duryea on the one hand, and De Dion, Benz, and Bernardi on the other was that the former were in essence and sometimes in fact horse carriages with engines attached, while the latter set out to create something entirely new: a motor-car as an independent entity on its own, owing nothing to the horse; though the Benz and Bernardi cars followed established stationary power transmission practice in primary drive by belts and change-speed pulleys (Benz), and bicycle practice in final drive by chain and in tubular chassis frames and wire-spoked road wheels (both cars). The latter line of development won, inevitably. The cars that succeeded in gaining public support were the ones that worked best, and these were the ones built specifically for the job, not mechanical compromises.

Yet, two qualifications to the generalization just made, which implies steady, inevitable progress, must be allowed. Technical changes, not all of them improvements, came slowly and patchily and in great variety, not tidily in one great enlightenment. The designers

4

were feeling their way in largely unknown territory. Their prior experience lay in very different fields—horse-carriage practice, steam, bicycle manufacture, stationary power for factories. They contended not only with new methods, but with new materials (or old ones that might or might not be suitable for the new medium)—the strength and powers of heat diffusion of steels and alloys; the problem of making efficient pneumatic tyres that would stand up to unprecedentedly high speeds on rough roads; and so forth. While general trends were in certain directions, experiment was the rule: this was a period of exploration in a new medium, of settling down. Anything went, in the metaphorical if not always in the literal sense. Three or four wheels; gasoline, steam, or electricity, or combinations; air or water cooling (or both); suspension non-existent, independent (12, 24, 25) or non-independent by leaf or coil springs; engines in front, back, or middle, or attached to the wheels (39); drive to the front (28) or back wheels by gears, shafts, chains, or belts, and permutations thereon; hot-tube, coil, and battery, or magneto ignition; four-stroke and two-stroke engines with one, two, three, or four cylinders in horizontal, vertical, or vee formation, longitudinally or transversely mounted; pneumatic or solid tyres—these were merely the more normal variations on the theme. Ignorance was not all of it; some engineers such as Benz and Daimler were conservative by nature, or lacked the financial backing for major changes of policy. The irregularity of technical progress is easily illustrated. Among gasoline vehicles, the next

major step came in 1891 with the so-called *système* Panhard (differing basic designs were called 'systems' by the French) (13). The French owner of the Daimler patents, the firm of Panhard et Levassor, introduced Emile Levassor's new design with engine at the front (instead of at the rear or in the middle, where it had lived until now), driving the rear wheels through a friction clutch, sliding-pinion gear-change and chain drive. Apart from the chains, the basic layout of the conventional car for generations to come had arrived, although Levassor's reason was simply to obtain better weight distribution and adhesion for the steering road wheels, and the system, never universal, did not finally conquer until the end of the decade. It could be said that it had won after Benz, the most powerful arch-conservative, started offering dummy hoods in 1900 and the influential De Dion in 1901, and when Daimler dropped rear engines in 1900. By 1904 the battle had been won in America as well. Wilhelm Maybach, Daimler's designer, introduced the jet-type carburettor in 1893, replacing the old surface-type which could not give efficient air–gasoline mixture control and high engine speeds; though, again, Benz retained it up to around the turn of the century. De Dion, converted to internal combustion, attached the world's first really high-speed gasoline engine to a tricycle in 1895, and to an automobile in 1899, thus making the practical small car possible (32). There was now an engine small enough to fit it, but powerful enough to drive it at a useful speed. The absence of belt drive, with its attendant power losses and inability to cope with high revolutions,

5

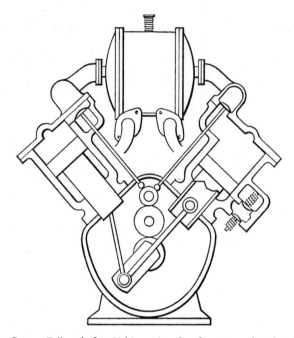

Fig. 4. Gustav Erikson's first Vabis engine, Sweden, 1897, elevation (see 20)

helped. The value of the De Dion engine was immediately appreciated and it was adopted by many manufacturers of automobiles from proprietary parts. Louis Renault in 1899 gave the small car its last major push to maturity by providing jointed shaft drive to a sprung live axle (54). It was generally held that only chains could transmit the power of a big engine, so shaft drive was not common on the largest cars for several years. It only became usual towards the end of the first decade of the new century.

In 1898–9, too, Simms-Bosch low-tension magneto ignition was making its appearance on Daimler (30), Mors (56), Benz (40), Nesselsdorf (38), Orient Express (27), and Turcat-Mery cars. Hot-tube ignition, with its burner-heated incandescent metal tube providing combustion, did not allow much variation in engine speeds, while battery and trembler-coil ignition, the other common system, depended on batteries that were at first too often unreliable. Still, hot-tube ignition, which was reliable except in windy or wet weather (when most motorists stayed at home) could be had on Panhards as late as 1902 (65). Panhard from 1898 quickly popularized the steering wheel on a raked column, which on Panhards but not all makes was by now combined with castor effect for self-centering action. The better-designed among the earliest automobiles had a single front wheel to avoid the instability inherent at any except the lowest speeds of the centre-pivot wagon-type steering normal with two front wheels. However, in 1891 Benz reintroduced Ackermann (or Lenkensperger)-type steering, which had been seen on steam road vehicles a couple of generations earlier, and two steered front wheels became a practical proposition. But conventional control was still by tiller, without self-centering action, and was dangerous at the increasing speeds becoming common. Panhard adopted wheel steering to take advantage of the speed potential of their machines. The same motive was behind their adoption of pneumatic tyres in the same year—solids were reliable, which pneumatics were not, but the vibration they set up knocked cars and drivers to pieces at speed.

The mechanically-operated inlet valve, which allowed still greater variation in engine speed, was seen in principle in the Markus, in the first Benz, and in the first Lanchester (23) of 1896, but did not catch on until adopted in the sensational new Mercedes-type Daimler devised by Wilhelm Maybach in 1901 (60). This feature spread very quickly. The modern honeycomb-type radiator of the Mercedes, with its myriad small tubes, had also been seen before, on a Daimler of 1899, but appearing now on a famous car, rendered obsolete the gilled (finned) tube radiator then universal. But, being expensive and fragile by comparison, it took longer to be generally taken up. The gilled-tube radiator was itself an improvement on the first form of water

cooling, consisting simply of circulation by pump to the engine's water jacket from a rear tank. A Daimler of 1899, too, had incorporated a pressed-steel chassis (much stronger than the conventional iron-reinforced wood frame), and a gate-type gear-change, which gave easier control by allowing changes to be made without going through all the intermediates, but again, it was the Mercedes of 1901, which also had these features, that propagated them because it was an incomparably better-known car. The steel frame, being an expensive item which needed special tooling to make, took a few years to become generally accepted.

The Mercedes was the last major landmark of the period, not because it was a mass of technical innovation, but because it managed to combine the most up to date and desirable features into a formula that made it a world leader, at first among expensive luxury cars and then among the rest. It was designed to be a thoroughly controllable, tractable fast car. No such thing had so far existed. Speed was provided by an enlarged version of a big four-cylinder engine of a type already seen in Daimlers. Four cylinders gave a smoother and more responsive flow of power than the more common one or two, and were seen in the bigger models of several manufacturers. The new engine had the full set of refinements incorporated for a wide range of flexibility in engine speed—low-tension magneto ignition, jet carburettor, mechanically-operated inlet valves. The gate-type gear-change allowed better use to be made of the fine engine, while the honeycomb radiator provided efficient

7

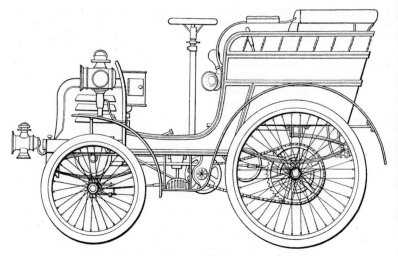

Fig. 5. The first F.N. car, Belgium, 1900, elevation

cooling. Stability was provided by a steel frame with a long wheelbase and low centre of gravity.

By this time, some steamers had reached a high pitch of technical sophistication and efficiency, but this brought complexity and expense in its train that were foreign to gasoline-engined cars, and the latter were still ahead when it came to speed of starting. Steam's advantages of comparative flexibility, smoothness, silence, and acceleration were secondary, though still potent enough in 1902 to carry on the battle. Electricity was nowhere, though offering these benefits as well, for short battery range and the need for constant skilled attention restricted electric cars to the towns. Here, in crowded traffic, their temporary advantages told, and in 1902 they were in their full, if limited, flowering.

However, more was necessary to the spread of the automobile's popularity than mere technical improvement. National character, economic conditions, and ease of existing communications had a lot to do with it. A Frenchman gave the initial impetus: the Germans brought the car to practical realization. But if the Germans gave it birth, the French provided the cradle. Benz, the first man to offer gasoline-engined vehicles to the public (1888), could not at first sell them in Germany. Technical virtuosity was there, not public interest. It was left to the enthusiastically empirical French, always willing to try innovations (most relevantly, the bicycle), to give motoring its just boost. They were helped by the excellence of the Napoleonic road system which, unlike British roads, had survived intact. Among the public of all countries, the real enemies were conservatism, and vested interests based on the horse and the railroad. The noise, smell, fumes, vibration, and unpredictability of most early automobiles in the hands of the tyro driver (into which category most drivers necessarily fell) were real enough, but the car's 'stinking, dirty, noisy, dangerous' characteristics were excuses for, or at most exacerbations of, deeper reasons for the new machine's early unpopularity, which arose in different countries at different times. In France, they were generally less strong than in Anglo-Saxon countries. Emile Roger, Emile Levassor of Panhard et Levassor, and Armand Peugeot (who used Panhard-type engines), all Frenchmen, first made a commercial proposition of selling the cars that had been created by the Germans Benz and Daimler (6, 9, 13).

Levassor, Bouton, and Louis Renault also improved upon them, making more sure of their wider acceptance, and it was the Comte de Dion and Alexandre Darracq (32, 55) who had the vision to bring improved vehicles within reach of a wide market for the first time, and to build them at the rate of over 1000 a year (both in 1901). However, it was the German, Wilhelm Maybach, who with the Mercedes-type Daimler (60), initiated a new period of technical progress and public acceptance, at a time when in his homeland, the automobile was still a curiosity. In this age, the British, their technical enterprise and public acceptance alike stifled by repressive legislation, usefully contributed only the first production six-cylinder car (Napier, 95), and the remarkable Lanchester (23, 83), an entirely original concept owing nothing to any practice established in other fields of engineering. It foreshadowed many important technical developments, but being outside the slower main stream, started no great trends itself. At the end of the period dealt with, the British motor industry was only just getting under way, led by Napier, Daimler, and Wolseley (44, 73, 86, 95), both the latter being makers of comparatively unadventurous motor-cars.

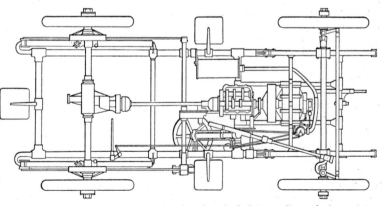

Fig. 6. Renault, France, 1901, plan showing shaft drive to live axle (see 54)

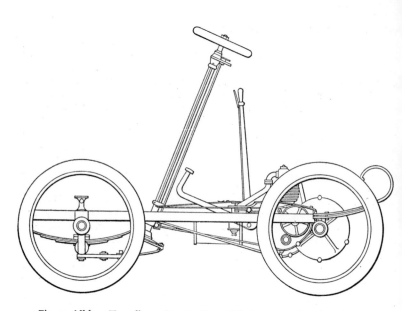

Fig. 7. Alldays Traveller *voiturette*, Great Britain, 1901, elevation (see 47)

Paradoxically, the American industry was in the same state, hampered not by legislation but by patent suits, and (mainly) by vast distances and lack of made roads outside the cities, which prevented a large market arising, and ensured that the cars made were generally simple and strong, but usually technically conservative vehicles of the horse-carriage 'gas buggy' type. However, by the end of the period American technical knowhow and foresight, running a little too far ahead of general conditions, had created the beginnings of quantity production in the motor industry (74, 75, 76, 88), on the principles already established in other industries in Britain and America—standardization and interchangeability of parts, and mass assembly. Skilled labour for traditional hand finishing was short, and its products were not uniform. The knowledge was there to design the machine tools needed to make the equipment needed to turn out parts to standard dimensions, and there was a mass of unskilled immigrant labour to hand, able and willing to do simple mass assembly. Darracq and De Dion in France each turned out 1200-odd cars in 1901, when Oldsmobile made 600, but then American production figures forged ahead (74, 75).

American and French outputs such as these were wholly exceptional. Their aim was to create demand by providing low-priced simplicity; they were not yet reflecting an existing demand. As will be seen in this book, normal production runs might be as few as six vehicles at a time, and a normal annual output fifty or fewer. Indeed, some manufacturers built cars one at a time, selling that before making another, or built only to order, in the manner of the carriage builders whose personnel and traditions they inherited. (The latter included technical features found in very early cars, such as centre-pivot steering, spoon brakes, and full-elliptic springs; and also body style nomenclature—phaeton, landaulet, dogcart, cabriolet, and the rest.) The typical workshop was staffed by slow, careful craftsmen working largely with hand tools, often to high standards of finish, and low standards of accuracy and uniformity. Restricted demand, low over-heads, and the acceptability of high prices in what was still a wealthy market, all allowing leisurely production, meant that even small concerns could afford to rely on their own, limited heavy plant, or make do with local foundries. Others with even less capital manufactured only the simplest parts, buying out engines (De Dion Bouton, Aster, Mutel, Buchet, and the rest), transmissions, and other parts more expensive and complex to build. They could do without the luxuries of specialized plant and specialist workmen. These assemblers were numerous also because of the prevalent ignorance of the art of motor manufacture. Of course, neither the typical manufacturer

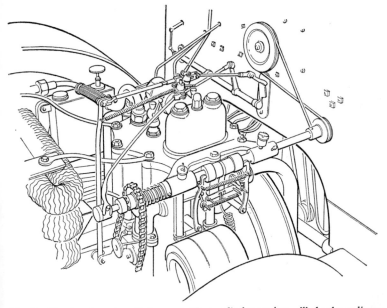

Fig. 8.   Marchand, 10 h.p., Italy, 1902. Two-cylinder engine, gilled-tube radiator (see 80)

nor the typical assembler could afford the specialized machine tools (which had themselves to be designed from scratch) or the large staffs necessary for the mass-production of uniform components, even if the demand had been there.

Countries such as Italy, Sweden, Switzerland, Belgium, and Austria, which were affected by one or more special conditions—small, predominantly agricultural populations, lack of cash or roads, or mountainous, wintry or forested terrain—had tiny industries that tended generally to copy other, leading countries' designs for lack of an engineering tradition and a pool of skilled workmen, or concentrated upon supplying the markets abroad that did not exist at home.

Generally, therefore, this was the picture in 1904. Technologically, thanks to French and German developments, the automobile had 'arrived' and in America and France the means for catering for a mass market had been evolved, against the time when that market opened up. Its general acceptance had begun, with France in the lead in this respect. It is no accident that, of around 100 types described in this book, which tries to give a balanced picture of the cars, mainstream and offbeat, of eleven countries, nearly 40 are French or directly French-derived, and over 20 German.

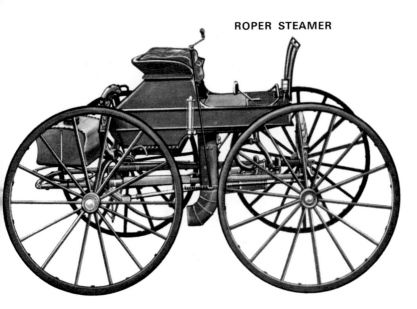

1

Roper Steamer. About 1863. U.S.A. Two horizontal cylinders, under seat. Charcoal-fired burner below rear-mounted generator. Water tank behind generator. Direct transmission. Tiller steering, centre pivot.

MARKUS

2

Markus. 1875 or 1877. Austria. Four-stroke rear engine, water cooled. Single horizontal cylinder, 100 × 200 mm., 1570 cc. Mechanically-operated slide inlet valve, poppet exhaust valve. Low-tension magneto ignition. Surface carburettor. Single forward speed. Metal to metal cone clutch, belt drive to solid rear axle. Slipping clutch differential adjacent to nearside rear hub. Final drive ratio 6.7:1. Centre-pivot steering. Shoe brakes.

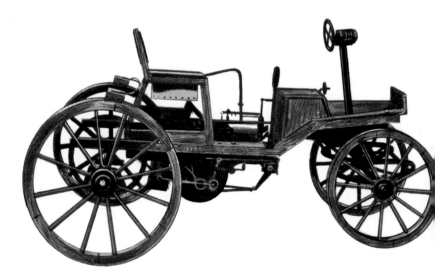

3

De Dion Bouton. 1885. France. Front vertical tubular generator, with condenser.
Automatic coke feed. Central engine, single cylinder. Water supply by mechanical
pump.

DAIMLER

4

Daimler. 1886. Germany. Four-stroke central engine, water cooled. Engine speed governed by control of exhaust valve opening. Single horizontal cylinder, 70 × 120 mm., 462 cc. Automatic inlet valve. Hot tube ignition. Primary drive by belt, final drive by pinions on countershaft engaging toothed rims on rear wheels. Centre-pivot steering.

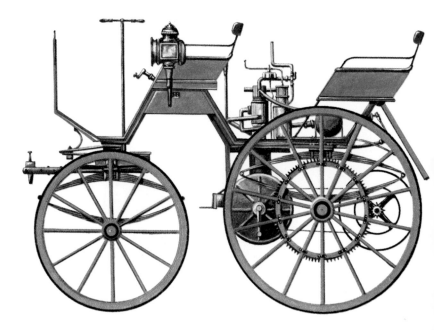

5

Hammel. 1886. Denmark. Rear four-stroke engine, water-cooled by pump. Two horizontal cylinders, 104.5 × 160 mm., 2720 cc. Automatic inlet valve. Hot-tube ignition. Surface carburettor. Double cone friction clutch, single constant-mesh forward speed, reverse speed. Chain final drive. Spoon brakes.

BENZ

6

Benz. About 1888. Germany. Rear four-stroke engine, water cooled by evaporation. Engine speed governed by mixture control. Single horizontal cylinder, 116 × 160 mm., 1600 cc. Mechanically-operated slide inlet valve, poppet exhaust valve. Battery and trembler coil ignition. Surface carburettor. Two forward speeds. Belt primary drive, chain final drive. Differential fitted.

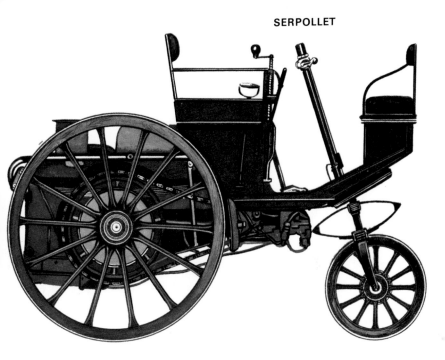

7

Serpollet. 1891. France. Flash generator, automatic coke feed. Two horizontal cylinders, under seat, 60.3 × 90.4 mm. Auxiliary water supply by hand pump. Two forward speeds, chain final drive.

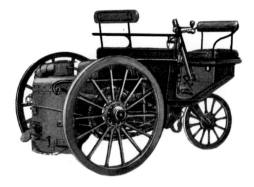

DURYEA

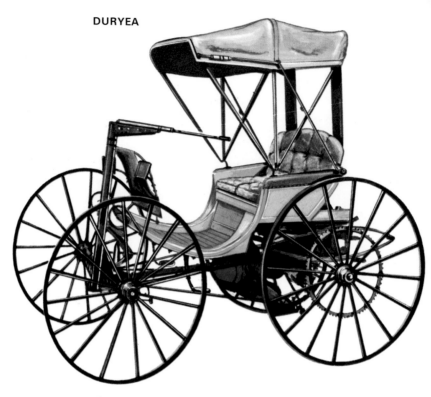

8

Duryea. 1893. U.S.A. Rear four-stroke engine. Single horizontal cylinder. Battery-operated low-tension ignition. Two forward speeds, gear transmission.

9

Peugeot. 1894. France. Rear four-stroke engine, water cooled. Two cylinders in vee formation, 80 × 120 mm., 1206 cc. Automatic inlet valves. Hot tube ignition. Surface carburettor. Four forward speeds. Cone clutch, sliding-pinion gearbox, chain final drive. Handlebar steering.

BREMER

10

Bremer. 1894. Great Britain. Rear four-stroke engine, water cooled by evaporation. Single horizontal cylinder, 600 cc. Battery and trembler coil ignition. Two forward speeds. Belt drive. Tiller steering. Spoon brakes.

11

Bernardi. 1894. Italy. Rear four-stroke engine, water cooled, gilled-tube radiator. Single horizontal cylinder, 85×110 mm., 624 cc. Overhead valves. Jet carburettor. Three forward speeds. Single chain final drive.

KNIGHT

12

Knight. 1895. Great Britain. Rear four-stroke engine, single cylinder, 114 × 152 mm., 1565 cc. Automatic inlet valve. Battery and trembler coil ignition. Two forward speeds, belt drive. Single shoe brake. Suspension by coil springs, independent at front.

13

Panhard-Levassor. 1895. France. Front four-stroke engine, 'Phoenix'-type, water cooled by evaporation. Engine speed governed by control of exhaust valve opening. Two vertical cylinders, 80 × 120 mm., 1206 cc. Automatic inlet valves. Hot-tube ignition. Jet carburettor. Three or four forward speeds. Double cone friction clutch, enclosed sliding-pinion gearbox, double chain final drive. Tiller steering.

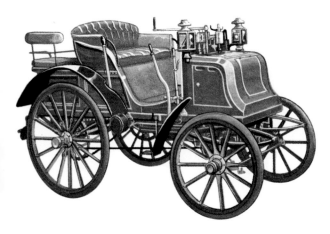

ROCHET-SCHNEIDER

14

Rochet-Schneider. 1895. France. Rear four-stroke engine. Single horizontal cylinder. Battery and trembler coil ignition. Two forward speeds. Belt primary drive, double chain final drive.

15

Lanza. 1895, 1898. Italy. Rear four-stroke engine, water cooled. Two horizontal cylinders. Hot-tube ignition. Two forward speeds (three forward speeds,
1898 phaeton, below). Cone clutch. Double chain final drive. Wheel steering.

PENNINGTON AUTOCAR

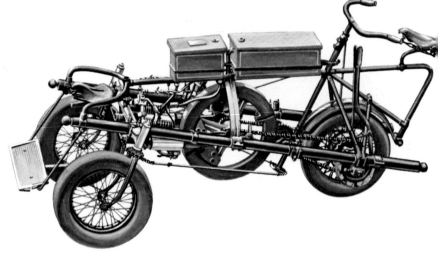

16

Pennington Autocar. 1896. Great Britain, U.S.A. Four-stroke engine. Two cylinders, 62.5 × 305 mm., 1868 cc. Automatic inlet valves. 'Long-mingling spark' ignition. No carburettor. Two-speed hub. Chain transmission. Handlebar steering. No road springs.

17

Thomson. 1896. Australia. Multi-tube generator, kerosene or paraffin burner under driver's seat. Tubular condenser. Front engine, two vertical cylinders, 76 × 76 mm. Two forward speeds. Belt primary drive, double chain final drive. Tiller steering.

FORD

18

Ford. 1896. U.S.A. Rear four-stroke engine. Two horizontal cylinders, 65 × 152.5 mm., 1050 cc. Two forward speeds. Belt primary and final drive. No differential. Tiller steering. Full-elliptic front springs, no rear springs. Tiller steering. Pneumatic tyres.

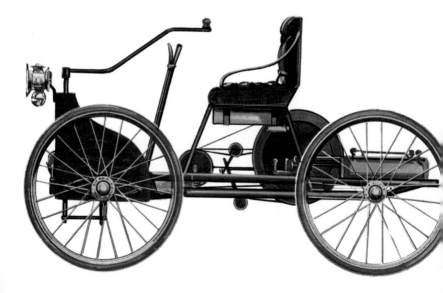

19

King. 1896. U.S.A. Four-stroke central engine, water cooled by evaporation. Four vertical cylinders in line. Coil and battery ignition. Belt primary drive, bevel final drive. Differential.

VABIS

20

Vabis. 1897. Sweden. Rear four-stroke engine, paraffin (kerosene) fuel, air cooled. Two horizontal cylinders. Automatic inlet valves. Low-tension magneto ignition. Then fitted with similar engine, hot-tube ignition; then with gasoline engine with two cylinders in vee formation. Two forward speeds. Epicyclic gearbox. Chain final drive. Tiller steering.

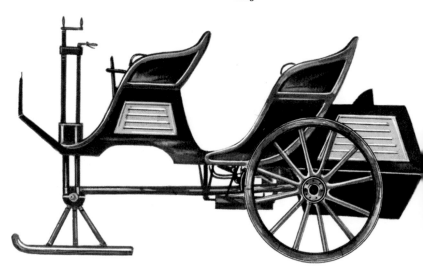

21

Vallée. 1897. France. Rear four-stroke engine, water cooled. Two horizontal cylinders, 100 × 200 mm., 3143 cc. Automatic inlet valve. Trembler coil and battery ignition. Surface carburettor. Three forward speeds. Belt primary drive, double chain final drive.

MENON

22

Menon. 1897. Italy. Front engine, water cooled cylinder head, air-cooled barrel, gilled tube radiator. Single vertical cylinder. Automatic inlet valve. Battery and trembler coil ignition. Two forward speeds. Belt primary and final drive.

23

Lanchester. 1897–1898. Great Britain. Rear engine, air cooled. Two horizontal cylinders, 127 × 115 mm., 2914 cc. Mechanically-operated inlet valves. Low-tension magneto ignition. Wick carburettor. Two forward speeds, epicyclic gearbox, direct drive on top gear. Live axle, worm final drive. Side lever steering.

STEPHENS

24

Stephens. 1898. Great Britain. Rear engine, water cooled by water jacket and radiator. Two horizontal cylinders, 90×152 mm., 1934 cc. Automatic inlet valves. Battery and trembler coil ignition. Surface carburettor. Two forward speeds. Belt primary drive, chain final drive. Independent front suspension. Tiller steering.

25

Decauville. 1898. France. Rear engine, air cooled. Two vertical cylinders, 66 × 70 mm., 479 cc. Automatic inlet valves. Battery and coil ignition. Surface carburettor. Two forward speeds. Cone clutch, sliding pinion gearbox, live axle. No rear suspension, independent front suspension. Tiller steering.

POPP

26

Popp. 1898. Switzerland. Rear engine, water cooled. Two horizontal cylinders, 90 × 122.5 mm., 1594 cc. Automatic inlet valves. Two forward speeds. Belt primary drive, chain final drive.

27

Orient Express. 1898. Germany. Rear engine, water cooled, by radiator. Single horizontal cylinder, 127 × 152 mm., 1800 cc. Automatic inlet valve. Low-tension magneto ignition. Three forward speeds. Belt primary drive (some friction drive?), chain final drive.

GRÄF

28

Gräf. 1898. Austria. Front engine, water cooled. Single vertical cylinder, 80 × 80 mm., 402 cc. Automatic inlet valve. Battery and coil ignition. Front wheel drive. Three forward speeds. Shaft drive.

STOEWER

29

Stoewer. 1899. Germany. Rear engine, water cooled. Two cylinders, 2100 cc. Battery and trembler coil ignition. Three forward speeds. Chain final drive.

30

Daimler. 1899. Germany. Rear engine, water-cooled. Two vertical cylinders, 90 × 130 mm., 1632 cc., transversely mounted. Automatic inlet valves. Hot-tube ignition. Jet carburettor. Four forward speeds. Belt primary drive, final drive by pinions on countershaft engaging toothed rims on rear wheels. Centre-pivot steering.

LÉON BOLLÉE

31

Léon Bollée. 1899. France. Rear engine, air-cooled. Engine speed governed by control of exhaust valve opening. Single horizontal cylinder, 76 × 145 mm., 650 cc. Automatic inlet valve. Hot-tube ignition. Jet carburettor. Three forward speeds. Belt final drive. No springs.

32

De Dion Bouton. 1899. France. Rear engine, water cooled. Single vertical cylinder, 80 × 80 mm., 402 cc. Automatic inlet valve. Battery and coil ignition. Jet carburettor. Two forward speeds. Epicyclic-type expanding-clutch gearbox. Final drive by gears to live axle. Handlebar steering.

GOBRON-BRILLIÉ

33

Gobron-Brillié. 1899. France. Rear engine, water cooled. Two transverse horizontal cylinders, four pistons, 80 × 80 mm., 1609 cc. Automatic inlet valves. Battery and trembler coil ignition. Three forward speeds. Cone clutch. Sliding pinion gearbox. Side chain final drive.

34

Prinetti & Stucchi. 1899. Italy. Front engine. Two vertical cylinders, 68 × 71 mm., 516 cc. Battery and trembler coil ignition. Two forward speeds. Belt drive.

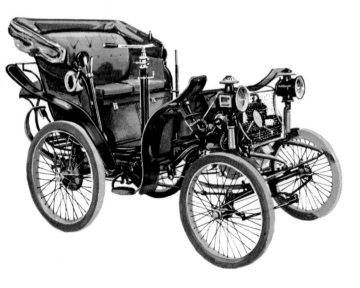

F.I.A.T.

35

F.I.A.T. 1899. Italy. Rear engine, water cooled, gilled-tube radiator. Two horizontal cylinders, 65 × 99 mm., 679 cc. Automatic inlet valves. Battery and trembler coil ignition. Surface carburettor. Three forward speeds. Cone clutch. Sliding pinion gearbox. Primary drive by gears to countershaft. Chain final drive. Handlebar steering.

DANSK AUTOMOBIL OG CYKEL FABRIK H. C. CHRISTIANSEN

36

Dansk Automobil og Cykel Fabrik H. C. Christiansen. About 1899. Denmark. Front engine, water cooled by evaporation. Single cylinder, 85 × 100 mm., 566 cc. Jet carburettor. Friction disc primary drive, single chain final drive. Tiller steering.

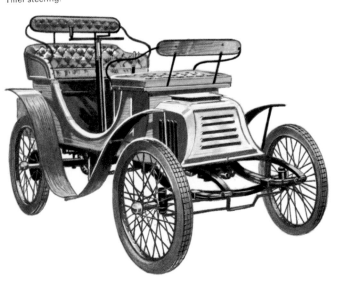

LOCOMOBILE

37

Locomobile. 1900. U.S.A. Rear vertical tubular generator, gasoline burner. Condenser on later cars. Under-seat engine, two vertical cylinders, 63 × 89 mm. Single chain drive to live rear axle.

38

Nesselsdorf. 1900. Austria. Central engine, water cooled by radiator and pump. Two horizontal cylinders, 120 × 120 mm., 2713 cc. Automatic inlet valves. Low-tension magneto ignition. Four forward speeds. Chain final drive. Handlebar steering.

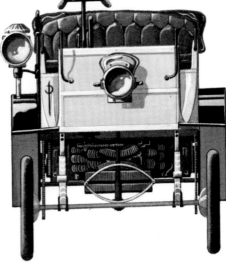

LOHNER-PORSCHE

39

Lohner-Porsche. 1900. Austria. Two electric motors in front wheel hubs. 40-cell, 135 amp/hour batteries. Three forward speeds, two reverse speeds. Wheel steering.

40

Benz. 1900. Germany. Rear engine, water cooled. Single horizontal cylinder, 110 × 110 mm., 1045 cc. Automatic inlet valve. Battery and trembler coil ignition. Surface carburettor. Three forward speeds. (Upper illustration: two forward speeds, 1894.) Belt primary drive, with Crypto epicyclic gear as emergency low. Chain final drive. Full-elliptic springs.

41

Adler. 1900. Germany. Front engine water cooled. Single vertical cylinder, 80×80 mm., 402 cc. Automatic inlet valve. Battery and coil ignition. Jet carburettor. Three forward speeds. Cone clutch, sliding pinion gearbox, shaft drive to live rear axle. Tiller steering.

42

Vivinus. 1900. Belgium. Front engine, air cooled. Single vertical cylinder, 95 × 100 mm., 785 cc. Automatic inlet valve. Battery and trembler coil ignition. Two forward speeds. Belt primary drive, belt and gear final drive (constant-mesh gearbox in rear axle).

ARGYLL

43

Argyll. 1900. Great Britain. Front engine, water cooled, gilled-tube radiator. Single vertical cylinder, 100×110 mm., 864 cc. Automatic inlet valve. Battery and trembler coil ignition. Three forward speeds. Cone clutch, sliding-pinion gearbox, shaft drive to live rear axle. Handlebar steering.

44

Napier. 1900. Great Britain. Front engine, water cooled by radiator and pump. Two vertical cylinders, 102 × 154 mm., 2450 cc. Automatic inlet valves. Battery and trembler coil ignition. Jet carburettor. Four forward speeds. Cone clutch, sliding-pinion gearbox, chain final drive.

ENGLISH MECHANIC

45

English Mechanic. 1900. Great Britain. Rear engine, water cooled. Single horizontal cylinder, 102 × 128 mm., 1026 cc. Mechanically-operated inlet valve. Battery and trembler coil ignition. Surface carburettor. Two forward speeds. Belt primary drive, chain final drive.

46

Royal Enfield Quad. 1901. Great Britain. Rear engine. Single vertical cylinder, 64 × 75 mm., 326 cc. or 80 × 80 mm., 402 cc. Automatic inlet valve. Battery and trembler coil ignition. Jet carburettor. Two forward speeds. Gear transmission.

ALLDAYS TRAVELLER

47

Alldays Traveller. 1901. Great Britain. Rear engine, air-cooled cylinder, water-cooled head. Single vertical cylinder, 64 × 75 mm., 326 cc. Automatic inlet valve. Jet carburettor. Battery and coil ignition. Two forward speeds. Cone clutch. Sliding-pinion gearbox. Spur gear final drive.

48

Sunbeam Mabley. 1901. Great Britain. Front engine, air-cooled cylinder barrel, water-cooled head. Single vertical cylinder, 64 × 75 mm., 326 cc. Automatic inlet valve. Battery and coil ignition. Two forward speeds. Belt primary drive, chain final drive to central driving axle. Tiller steering.

ALBION

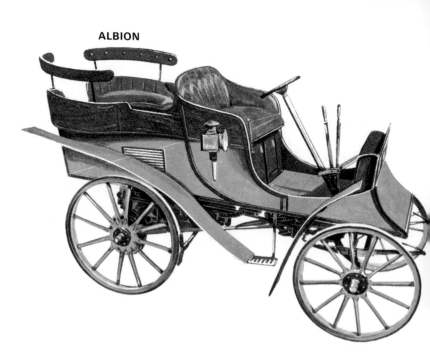

49

Albion. 1901. Great Britain. Rear engine, water cooled. Two horizontal cylinders, 102 × 128 mm., 2092 cc. Automatic inlet valves. Low-tension magneto ignition. Jet carburettor. Three forward speeds. Cone clutch. Single chain final drive. Tiller steering.

50

Arrol-Johnston. 1901. Great Britain. Rear engine water cooled. Two horizontal cylinders, four pistons, 108 × 83 mm., 3042 cc. Automatic inlet valves. Low-tension magneto ignition. Jet carburettor. Four forward speeds. Chain primary drive to cone clutch, single chain final drive. Wheel steering.

FRATELLI CEIRANO

51

Fratelli Ceirano. 1901. Italy. Front engine, water cooled. Single vertical cylinder, 86 × 110 mm., 639 cc. Automatic inlet valve. Jet carburettor. Three forward speeds. Cone clutch, shaft final drive.

52

Luc Court. 1901. France. Front engine, water cooled. Two cylinders. Low-tension magneto ignition. Jet carburettor. Cone clutch. Five forward speeds. Double chain final drive.

53

Corre. 1901. France. Front engine, water cooled. Single vertical cylinder, 90 × 100 mm., 634 cc. Automatic inlet valve. Jet carburettor. Three forward speeds. Cone clutch, shaft final drive.

RENAULT

54

Renault. 1901. France. Front engine, water cooled, gilled-tube radiator. Single vertical cylinder, 80 × 80 mm., 402 cc. Automatic inlet valve. Battery and coil ignition. Jet carburettor. Three forward speeds. Cone clutch, tumbler gearbox, shaft drive to live axle. Wheel steering.

DARRACQ

55

Darracq. 1901. France. Front engine, water cooled. Single vertical cylinder, 100 × 100 mm., 786 cc. Automatic inlet valve. Battery and trembler coil ignition. Jet carburettor. Three forward speeds. Cone clutch. Sliding-pinion gearbox. Shaft final drive to live axle.

56

Mors. 1901. France. Front engine, air-cooled cylinder barrels, water-cooled heads. Four vertical cylinders, 80 × 120 mm., 2414 cc. Automatic inlet valves. Low-tension magneto ignition. Four forward speeds. Cone clutch. Chain final drive.

CLÉMENT GLADIATOR

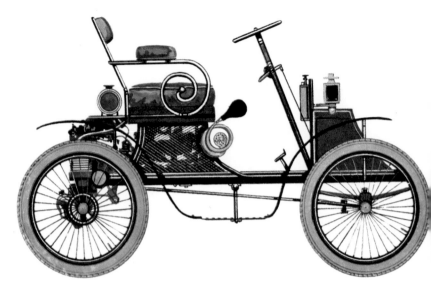

57

Clément Gladiator. 1901. France. Rear engine, water cooled cylinder head, air cooled cylinder barrel. Single vertical cylinder, 64 × 75 mm., 326 cc. Automatic inlet valve. Battery and coil ignition. Two forward speeds. Direct drive by gearing. Wheel steering.

DELAHAYE

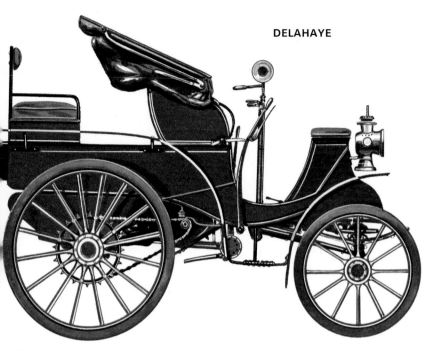

58

Delahaye. 1901. France. Rear engine, water cooled. Single horizontal cylinder, 110×160 mm., 1521 cc. Automatic inlet valve. Battery and trembler coil ignition. Surface carburettor. Two forward speeds. Belt primary drive, chain final drive. Handlebar steering.

SCANIA

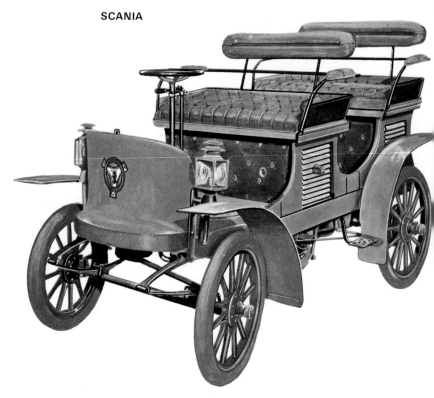

59

Scania. 1901. Sweden. Central engine, air cooled. Single transverse horizontal cylinder. Epicyclic gearbox. Chain final drive. Wheel steering.

MERCEDES

60

Mercedes. 1901. Germany. Front engine, water cooled, honeycomb radiator. Four vertical cylinders, 116 × 140 mm., 5900 cc. Mechanically-operated inlet valves. Low-tension magneto ignition. Jet carburettor. Four forward speeds. Cone clutch, sliding-pinion gearbox, chain final drive.

MAURER UNION

61

Maurer Union. 1901. Germany. Front engine, water cooled. Single cylinder, 110 × 120 mm., 1140 cc. Automatic inlet valve. Low-tension magneto ignition. Jet carburettor. Two forward speeds. Single friction disc primary drive, single chain final drive.

62

Durkopp. 1901. Germany. Front engine, water cooled. Two vertical cylinders, 94 × 130 mm., 1804 cc. Automatic inlet valves. Low-tension magneto and coil ignition. Jet carburettor. Three forward speeds. Cone clutch. Sliding-pinion gearbox. Side chain final drive.

COLUMBIA

63

Columbia. 1901. U.S.A. Front engine, water cooled. Single vertical cylinder, 117×174 mm., 1871 cc. Battery and trembler coil ignition. Three forward speeds. Cone clutch. Sliding pinion gearbox. Live axle.

KNOX

64

Knox. 1901. U.S.A. Central engine, air cooled. Single horizontal cylinder, 115 × 153 mm., 1600 cc. Two forward speeds. Epicyclic gearbox. Mechanically-operated inlet valve. Battery and trembler coil ignition. Single chain final drive. Tiller steering.

PANHARD-LEVASSOR

65

Panhard-Levassor 6–7 h.p. 1902. France. Two vertical cylinders, 90 × 130 mm., 1632 cc. Water-cooled, gilled-tube radiator and pump. Engine speed governed by mixture control. Automatic inlet valves. Battery and trembler coil ignition, or hot-tube ignition, or both. Three or four forward speeds. Cone clutch. Chain final drive. Wheel steering.

GEORGES RICHARD

Georges Richard. 1902. France. Front engine, water cooled. Two vertical cylinders 90 × 110 mm., 1396 cc. Automatic inlet valve. Jet carburettor. Battery and coil ignition. Three forward speeds. Cone clutch, sliding-pinion gearbox, shaft final drive.

PEUGEOT

67

Peugeot. 1902. France. Front engine, water cooled. Single vertical cylinder, 94 × 94 mm., 695 cc. Automatic inlet valve. Battery and trembler coil ignition. Two forward speeds. Cone clutch. Shaft final drive to live axle.

68

Gillet-Forest. 1902. France. Front engine, steam cooled. Engine speed governed by control of exhaust valve opening. Single horizontal transverse cylinder, 127 × 140 mm., 1775 cc. Automatic inlet valve. Battery and trembler coil ignition. Three forward speeds. Cone clutch. Shaft final drive to live axle.

DE DIETRICH

69

De Dietrich. 1902. France. Front engine, water cooled. Four vertical cylinders, 104 × 120 mm., 4080 cc. Automatic inlet valves. Jet carburettor. Low-tension magneto ignition. Four forward speeds. Cone clutch. Chain final drive.

70

Ader. 1902. France. Front engine, water cooled. Two cylinders in vee formation, 80 × 90 mm., 905 cc. Automatic inlet valves. Battery and trembler coil ignition. Wick carburettor. Three forward speeds. Cone clutch. Sliding-pinion gearbox. Chain final drive.

BERNA

71

Berna. 1902. Switzerland. Rear engine, water cooled. Single vertical cylinder, 100×100 mm., 785 cc. Automatic inlet valve. Battery and coil ignition. Two forward speeds. Epicyclic-type expanding-clutch gearbox. Final drive by gears to live axle.

WEBER

72

Weber. 1902. Switzerland. Rear engine, water cooled. Two horizontal cylinders.
Automatic inlet valves. Belt drive.

WOLSELEY

73

Wolseley. 1902. Great Britain. Front engine, water cooled. Two horizontal cylinders, 114 × 127 mm., 2605 cc. Automatic inlet valves. Battery and trembler coil ignition. Four forward speeds. Cone clutch in flywheel. Chain primary drive to sliding-pinion gearbox. Chain final drive.

74

Oldsmobile. 1902. U.S.A. Rear engine, water cooled. Single horizontal cylinder, 114.3 × 152.4 mm., 1565 cc. Mechanical inlet valve. Battery and trembler coil ignition. Two forward speeds. Epicyclic gearbox. Single chain final drive. Tiller steering.

RAMBLER

75

Rambler. 1902. U.S.A. Central engine, water cooled. Single horizontal cylinder, 127 × 152.4 mm., 1931 cc. Mechanically-operated inlet valve. Battery and trembler coil ignition. Two forward speeds. Epicyclic gearbox. Single chain final drive to live axle. Tiller steering.

76

Winton. 1902. U.S.A. Central engine, water cooled. Engine speed governed by pneumatic control of inlet valve opening. Two horizontal cylinders, 134 × 153 mm., 4443 cc. Automatic inlet valves. Two jet carburettors. Battery and trembler coil ignition. Two forward speeds. Single chain drive to live axle.

PACKARD

77

Packard. 1902. U.S.A. Central transverse engine, water cooled. Single hori-
zontal cylinder, 153 × 165 mm., 3035 cc. Automatic inlet valve. Jet carburettor.
Battery and trembler coil ignition. Three forward speeds. Epicyclic gearbox.
Single chain final drive to live axle.

78

Baker. 1902. U.S.A. Central Elwell-Parker electric motor. Twelve 2-volt, 70 amp/hour batteries. Three forward speeds. Central chain drive to live axle. Tiller steering.

F.I.A.T.

79

F.I.A.T. 1902. Italy. Front engine, water cooled. Four vertical cylinders, 100 × 120 mm., 3770 cc. Automatic inlet valves. Jet carburettor. Low-tension magneto ignition. Three forward speeds. Cone clutch. Chain final drive.

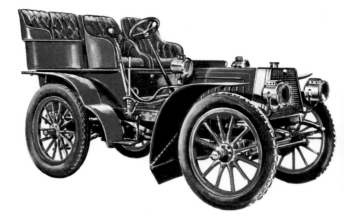

80

Marchand. 1902. Italy. Front engine, water cooled. Two vertical cylinders, 97 × 105 mm., 1552 cc. Automatic inlet valves. Low-tension magneto ignition. Three forward speeds. Chain final drive.

WARTBURG

81

Wartburg. 1902. Germany. Rear engine, water cooled. Two vertical cylinders, 87 × 95 mm., 1100 cc. Automatic inlet valves. Battery and trembler coil ignition. Two forward speeds. Cone clutch. Shaft drive to live rear axle. Independent front suspension, half-elliptic rear suspension.

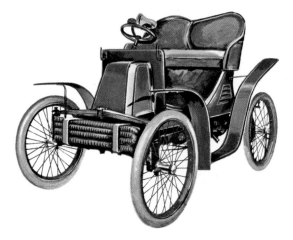

GLADIATOR

Gladiator. 1903. France. Front engine, water cooled. Two vertical cylinders, 105 × 130 mm., 2230 cc. Automatic inlet valves. Battery and trembler coil ignition. Three forward speeds. Cone clutch. Chain final drive.

LANCHESTER

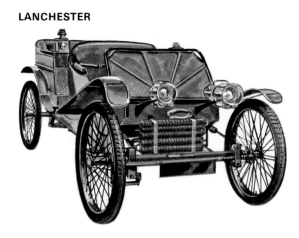

83

Lanchester. 1903. Great Britain. Central engine, air cooled. Two horizontal cylinders, 134 × 145 mm. 3900 cc. Mechanically-operated inlet valves. Low-tension magneto ignition. Wick carburettor. Three forward speeds, epicyclic gearbox, direct drive on top gear. Live axle, worm final drive. Side lever steering.

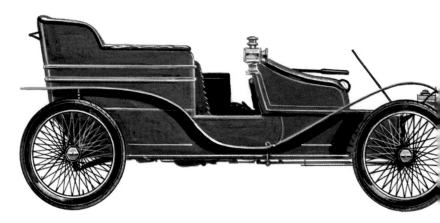

84

Standard. 1903. Great Britain. Front engine, water cooled. Single vertical cylinder, 127 × 76 mm., 963 cc. Mechanically-operated inlet valve. Battery and trembler coil ignition. Three forward speeds. Cone clutch. Shaft drive to live axle.

HUMBERETTE

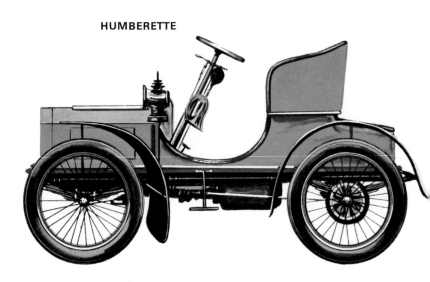

85

Humberette. 1903. Great Britain. Front engine, water cooled. Single vertical cylinder, 92.2 × 92.2 mm., 615 cc. Automatic inlet valve. Battery and trembler coil ignition. Two forward speeds. Cone clutch. Shaft drive to live axle.

86

Daimler. 1903. Great Britain. Front engine, water cooled. Four vertical cylinders, 105 × 130 mm., 4503 cc. Automatic inlet valves. Dual ignition by hot tube and battery and coil. Four forward speeds. Cone clutch. Chain final drive.

CADILLAC

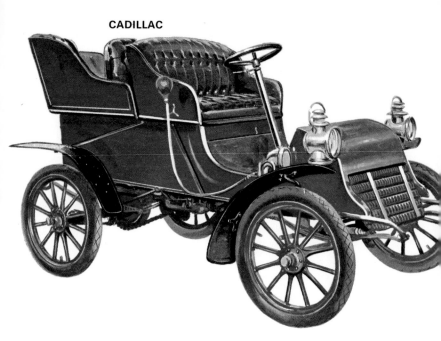

87

Cadillac. 1903. U.S.A. Central engine, water cooled. Single horizontal transverse cylinder, 127 × 127 mm., 1700 cc. Mechanically-operated overhead inlet valve. Coil and battery ignition. Epicyclic gearbox. Two forward speeds. Central chain drive to live axle.

88

Ford. 1903. U.S.A. Central engine, water cooled. Two horizontal transverse cylinders, 102 × 102 mm., 1668 cc. Mechanically-operated inlet valve. Coil and battery ignition. Epicyclic gearbox. Two forward speeds. Central chain drive to live axle.

DURYEA

89

Duryea. 1903. U.S.A. Central engine, water cooled. Three inclined transverse cylinders, 102 × 152 mm., 3727 cc. Automatic inlet valves; then mechanically-operated inlet valves. Low-tension flywheel magneto ignition. Epicyclic gearbox on rear axle. Two forward speeds. Central chain drive to live rear axle.

90

Franklin. 1903. U.S.A. Front engine, air cooled. Four vertical transverse cylinders, 83 × 83 mm., 1800 cc. Automatic inlet valves, mechanically-operated overhead exhaust valves. Trembler coil and battery ignition. Epicyclic gearbox. Two forward speeds. Single chain drive to rear axle.

SCANIA

91

Scania. 1903. Sweden. Front engine, water cooled. Two vertical cylinders. Automatic inlet valves. Battery and trembler coil or low-tension magneto ignition. Two or three forward speeds. Chain final drive.

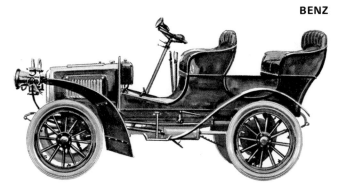

92

Benz. 1903. Germany. Front engine, water cooled. Two vertical cylinders, 90 × 120 mm., 1527 cc. Automatic inlet valves. Low-tension magneto ignition. Three forward speeds. Cone clutch. Shaft drive.

93

Benz. 1903. Germany. Front engine, water cooled. Four vertical cylinders, 90 × 110 mm., 2800 cc. Automatic inlet valves. Low-tension magneto ignition. Three forward speeds. Cone clutch. Shaft drive.

GARDNER-SERPOLLET

94

Gardner-Serpollet. 1904. France. Flash generator, automatic feed of water to generator and oil to burner by donkey engine. Front engine, four horizontal cylinders, 78 × 78 mm. Shaft final drive to live axle.

95

Napier. 1904. Great Britain. Front engine, water cooled. Six vertical cylinders, 101 × 101 mm., 3238 cc. Mechanically-operated overhead inlet valves. Battery and coil ignition. Three forward speeds. Chain final drive.

ROYCE

96

Royce. 1904. Great Britain. Front engine, water cooled. Two vertical cylinders, 95 × 127 mm., 1800 cc. Mechanically-operated overhead inlet valves. Battery and trembler coil ignition. Three forward speeds. Cone clutch. Shaft drive to live axle.

97

Vauxhall. 1903–1904. Great Britain. Front engine, water cooled. Single transverse horizontal cylinder, 101 × 120 mm., 962 cc. Automatic inlet valve. Battery and trembler coil ignition. Epicyclic gearbox. Two forward speeds. Single chain drive to live rear axle. Coil spring suspension at front and rear. Tiller steering.

ROVER

98

Rover. 1904. Great Britain. Front engine, water cooled. Single vertical cylinder, 114 × 130 mm., 1300 cc. Mechanically-operated overhead inlet valve. Battery and trembler coil or high-tension magneto ignition. Three forward speeds. Plate clutch. Shaft drive to rear axle.

PASSENGER CARS IN DETAIL

1 ROPER STEAMER, about 1863, U.S.A.

The steam vehicle illustrated was one of the earliest, if not the earliest, mechanically-propelled light passenger vehicles for personal transportation—a 'motorcar' in the proper sense—to be built in the U.S.A. It survives, and is housed in the Henry Ford Museum, Dearborn, Michigan. Sylvester H. Roper of Roxbury, Massachusetts had made a steam-driven velocipede that appeared at fairs and circuses in New England, in competition with horses. At about the same time, he also built the four-wheeled steam carriage shown. It was no more than a conventional high-wheeled buggy modified for steam propulsion. Power output was 2 b.h.p., the weight of the complete vehicle was around 6 cwt., and its maximum speed was around 20 m.p.h. Its external resemblance to the high-wheeled buggy-type gasoline-engined cars that enjoyed a brief vogue in America forty or fifty years later is obvious. Roper was America's most prolific early constructor of steam vehicles. By 1895 he had built ten, two of which still exist: the buggy shown, and a tricycle, which is in the Smithsonian Institution in Washington, D.C.

2 MARKUS, 1875 or 1877, Austria

The car illustrated, which still exists in running order in the Technisches Museum für Industrie und Gewerbe in Vienna, is claimed to be the world's first internal-combustion-engined vehicle to run successfully. Siegfried Markus, a naturalized Austrian of German birth, was a prolific inventor, for the most part of electrical devices. He built a first, extremely primitive vehicle around 1864, but there is no suggestion that it ran. His second car, which is illustrated, was ahead of its time in some ways, with its mechanically-operated inlet valve, detachable cylinder-head, and low-tension magneto ignition that foreshadowed the later Simms-Bosch type. Performance was feeble in the extreme, understandably since an engine developing three-quarters of one horsepower at 500 r.p.m. was expected to pull $14\frac{1}{2}$ cwt. The maximum speed was 4–5 m.p.h. The car worked, even so, but nothing came of it. Markus did not see any commercial possibilities in it, and would not have been excited if he had, because he was a pure amateur who lost interest in his inventions once they functioned to his satisfaction.

3 DE DION BOUTON, 1885, France

In 1883 there began the association of the Comte de Dion with Georges Bouton and Trépardoux, engineers. The latter pair built for the Count a series of steam road vehicles, concentrating upon the light passenger machines in which De Dion was primarily interested. He became the first manufacturer in Europe to embark upon manufacture of vehicles of this type, though they were never in serious production. The first car was a quadricycle with front-wheel drive by belts, and rear-wheel steering. Others followed, including the tricycle illustrated, which is preserved in the Conservatoire National in Paris. This machine had two front steering wheels, and one rear driving wheel. Boiler and water-tank were between the front wheels. The capacity of the coke hoppers on either side of the rear wheel gave the little car a range of three-quarters of an hour's running, and the maximum speed was said to be between 15 and 20 m.p.h. Two quadricycles were the runners in the contest held by the journal *Le Velocipède* in 1887. The Pecori steamer of 1891, from Italy, was based on a De Dion-Bouton design. De Dion and Bouton built the gasoline road vehicles for which they became famous from 1895, finally dropping steamers four years later.

4 DAIMLER, 1886, Germany

Otto & Langen's four-stroke stationary gas engine of 1876, inspired by Lenoir's engine of 1860, was made in their factory at Deutz. Gottlieb Daimler, its designer, had seen Lenoir engines at work, and while in England had been consulting engineer to Crossley, makers of the Otto engine there. In 1872 he had become technical director of Otto & Langen, and remained in this position for ten years. Wilhelm Maybach, the chief designer, put his ideas into practice, then as later. Daimler, like Karl Benz, saw the need for an internal-combustion engine that could be used as a power unit for various means of mechanical transportation, and like

Benz, chose gasoline as a suitably portable fuel not tied to gas-mains. Such an engine must be compact and light, so would have to develop a lot of power for its size. The answer lay in higher engine speeds. In 1882 Daimler set up on his own in Cannstatt, and built his first such engine in the following year. In 1885 he built an experimental motor-cycle, and in 1886 had a motor carriage on the road. It was literally a horse carriage, with an engine and transmission fitted. The Daimler engine, thanks to its hot-tube ignition, devised by Daimler, would run up to 900 r.p.m., and gave 1.1 b.h.p. at 650 r.p.m.

At the time electric ignition was unreliable, and the flame ignition of the gas engine forbade high engine speeds. Daimler's engines were fitted to a boat in 1886, to a rail vehicle in 1887, and to an airship in 1888—he was not yet specially interested in motor-cars. A year later, however, Daimler built another 1886-type vehicle, and also his first motor-car proper—designed as such from the ground up. This machine was very precocious. It had a new vee-twin engine that was smaller but was lighter and gave more power ($3\frac{1}{2}$ b.h.p.), and which had a water-jacket and pump for better cooling. The frame was of steel tube. There were four forward speeds through a cone friction clutch, and a bevel-gear differential. Steering was on Ackermann principles, and a drum brake was fitted. This modern machine, the so-called 'Steel Wheel Car', was another experiment, which did not go into production. Daimler and Maybach left the Daimler Motoren Gesellschaft in 1890 to act as consultants, and until they returned five years later, not more than a dozen cars left Cannstatt. But these did include technical innovations which were carried over into the production cars made from 1895. A lighter, more efficient two-cylinder in-line engine was introduced in 1892, and in 1893 the Maybach jet carburettor—the modern instrument in principle—arrived.

By 1895, too, the name of Daimler was well established abroad. Emile Levassor had controlled the Daimler patents in France since 1890, and his firm, Panhard et Levassor, had been building independently-designed cars round the engine since the same year. In 1891, Frederick R. Simms, an English director of the Daimler Motoren Gesellschaft, acquired the British rights in the Daimler patents, and five years later sold them to H. J. Lawson's British Motor Syndicate, which had been floated partly to make Daimler cars (86). In the same year of 1895, a company was founded at Turin to build Daimler cars under licence in Italy. In 1888, William Steinway, the piano manufacturer, had gained the American rights in the Daimler engine. At first he assembled them from imported parts, but in 1891 produced the first American-built Daimler engine. From 1893 Steinway imported complete cars. They were shown at the Chicago World's Fair of that year, which Gottlieb Daimler visited.

5 HAMMEL, 1886, Denmark

Denmark's first car is claimed as a contemporary of the other pioneers from Germany, the Daimler (4) and Benz (6), but unlike them, it did not lead anywhere. Its constructor was Hans Urban Johansen, a blacksmith in the workshop of Albert F. Hammel. Johansen is known to have seen the Otto stationary engine, and it seems likely that he had also either seen, or seen described, the Daimler car. The Hammel's engine was large in comparison, however, and developed between $2\frac{1}{2}$ and $3\frac{1}{2}$ b.h.p. Maximum speed was around 6 m.p.h. The steering was strange, in that it was turned against the direction required. The car was driven twelve miles a day regularly for two years, between Copenhagen and Skovshoved, where Johansen lived, but only one was ever built. It still exists, in the Danish Technical Museum, and is in running order.

6 BENZ, about 1888, Germany

With the Austrian Markus car, and (possibly) the Danish Hammel, the German Benz and Daimler cars were the earliest internal-combustion-engined road vehicles to run successfully. The first Benz was the true progenitor of the modern motor industry, since its development was definitely the world's first gasoline-engined car to go into commercial production. Benz was a practical manufacturer as well as an engineer. While a student in 1861, Karl Benz saw a Lenoir stationary gas engine at work. He built his own two-stroke gas engine in 1877, putting it into production five years later. By 1886 the Otto four-stroke patent was void, so Benz began making four-stroke stationary gas engines as well. He had already designed a gasoline-engined road vehicle—as an entity, not just as a horse carriage with an engine attached like the first Daimler. It was built in 1885 and running a year later. In this, and its electric ignition and mechanically-operated (slide) inlet valve, it was ahead of its time. The engine developed between two-thirds and nine-tenths of one horsepower, at between 250 and 400 r.p.m., which sufficed to drive it at up to 10 m.p.h. Steering was by a single front wheel, as Benz disliked the centre-pivot steering common to horse-drawn vehicles, which was dangerous at speed. Although the Librarian of the Imperial Patent Office said that 'the internal-combustion engine has as little future as steam for motivating road vehicles', the little car ran successfully in the streets of Mannheim during 1886. Benz built at least another two similar cars in 1888, and began to catalogue them for sale along with his separate engines. They could be had with wire wheels, as on the original car, or with artillery-type wheels, as illustrated. The machine illustrated still exists in the Science Museum in London. It differs from the first Benz in (among other things) having a larger engine of $1\frac{1}{2}$ h.p., and front seats. Nobody in Germany was interested, but in 1889 Emile Roger, a French customer for Benz stationary engines, bought a car. He became the Paris agent for Benz cars, and later assembled them from imported parts. In the following year, Benz acquired more capital, and from 1891 to 1893 the Rheinische Gasmotoren Fabrik began to make cars more seriously—though stationary engines were still its main stock-in-trade. These cars had two forward speeds, with two driving belts, and a horizontal instead of vertical fly-wheel. The first major mechanical

alterations, however, came in a proto-type of 1891, which had four wheels and Ackermann (or Lenkensperger) rack-and-pinion steering, which allowed faster, safer motoring since two steering road wheels were now possible without the dangerous centre-pivot steering. This design, with an automatic inlet valve, and a float feed (providing constant fuel feed, abolishing the need for continual refilling of the carburettor), was offered for sale from 1893. The enlarged engine had a bore and stroke of 130 by 150 mm., giving 2 litres, 3 b.h.p. at 470 r.p.m., and 14 m.p.h. This Benz Victoria, as the design was called, was one of the first production cars. At the same time, the brilliant engineer August Horch arrived to work with Benz, and the company was ready to move into a new world. The first Benz seen in Britain arrived in 1894, and a year later the make was entered in the *Chicago Times–Herald* Thanksgiving Day Race.

7 SERPOLLET, 1891, France

The ambition of Léon Serpollet was to produce a truly efficient light personal steam carriage. As early as 1885 he had devised his 'flash' generator, which was light in weight because it was compact. Water was pumped into a heated, multi-coiled pipe, where it was instantly converted ('flashed') into superheated steam. The system had other advantages: it was quick, it was economical (in that water was heated only when it was actually generating steam), it allowed easy control, since steam pressure was regulated by the amount of water entering the generator, and it was safe, for there being little water at any time in the generator, the possibility of an explosion was remote. In 1887 Serpollet fitted his engine to his first road vehicle, a tricycle, which worked well. A passenger vehicle with a more powerful engine followed, that was the subject of army trials. Les Fils de Peugeot Frères of Valentigney, an iron-mongery firm, had diversified into bicycles in 1885. Four years later, Serpollet, in conjunction with Armand Peugeot, built in the bicycle factory a three-wheeled car which in 1890 he drove from Paris to Lyons with Ernest Archdeacon. The journey of 290 miles took two weeks. However, by the end of that year Serpollet was sufficiently confident in his product to put it into limited production. About twelve were built in 1891, one for Gaston Menier of the chocolate family. Another was exported to India. They were four-passenger machines capable of an excellent performance when compared with gasoline-engined vehicles of the day, with their 4–6 b.h.p. and maximum speed of about 16 m.p.h. In the low gear, they could climb a gradient of 1 : 7 fully laden. The fuel range was eighteen miles, and the water range double that. The controls were simple, consisting of a steering lever with a twist-grip that controlled the water supply. The latter could be boosted by an auxiliary hand pump. Fuelling was automatic, from hoppers. During 1891, a four-wheeler with Ackermann steering was introduced, but Armand Peugeot had already withdrawn his support, because by now he was working on a car of his own, gasoline powered (8). For the next seven years, Serpollet abandoned passenger cars,

turning to the application of his engine to trams and railcars.

8 DURYEA, 1893, U.S.A.

Until and unless the claims of the 1891 Lambert are proved, Charles Edgar Duryea remains as the man primarily responsible for America's first working internal-combustion-engined road vehicle. Charles and his brother Frank were bicycle mechanics. He built his first gasoline engine in 1886, and three years later read about the Benz cars from Germany in the *Scientific American*. In 1893 his first complete car was running in Springfield, Massachusetts. It was nothing but a horse buggy with an engine, like the first Daimler, and like that car, was an experiment. Illustrated here, it had a single-cylinder engine and two forward speeds. The brothers were encouraged by its success to form the Duryea Motor Wagon Company at Peoria, Illinois, in 1894—the first company in America to be founded for the purpose of making motor vehicles. The second Duryea, with its two cylinders and three forward speeds, was an improvement on the first. This was the machine that won the 54-mile *Chicago Times–Herald* Race from Chicago to Evanston and back, America's first motor race, on Thanksgiving Day, 1895. The Duryeas now went into production, making thirteen cars during 1896. Two crossed the Atlantic to take part in the London–Brighton Emancipation Run of November that year; a very early instance of showing the flag. Both appear to have finished, in spite of prejudiced reports. These machines used belt primary drive and gear final drive, instead of all-gear transmission, and were fully sprung, whereas the Chicago race car was sprung only at the front. Now the brothers parted, to quarrel over the credit for their first car, and the company stagnated. It died in 1898, but was revived as the Duryea Power Company of Waterloo, Iowa. For several years thereafter the staple model was characterized by a transverse, inclined, three-cylinder engine with *désaxé* crankshaft (a feature it pioneered), 'one-hand' control by means of a lever that tilted to steer, twisted to operate the throttle, and pushed down to change gear, and some elegant, comfortable bodies in opulent curvilinear shapes that tried to conceal the ingenious motor-car beneath. The firm's last product was the extremely *in*elegant Buggyaut high-wheeler, which was made as late as 1913. Convention was against the Duryea; even the British Duryea Company, founded in 1904, which made a range of its own models as well, was a failure.

9   PEUGEOT, 1894, France

Les Fils de Peugeot Frères, makers of ironmongery, diversified into the bicycle field in 1885. Four years later, at the instance of Armand Peugeot, Léon Serpollet's first full-scale three-wheeled steam car was built in the cycle factory (7). A few were made during 1890–1, and a four-wheeler was also constructed, but around this time Armand Peugeot withdrew from his association with Serpollet, for he was working on a gasoline car. By 1891 it was on the road; in fact, it successfully followed the course of the Paris–Brest bicycle race of that year. By 1891–2 the new

machine was in production; therefore becoming the first French car to achieve this status. Peugeot utilized a vee-twin engine as made by Panhard & Levassor under licence from Daimler (13) and the transmission, by cone clutch, sliding-pinion gear-box and chains, was on Panhard-Levassor lines, but otherwise Peugeot's first gasoline car was quite different from its contemporary. It was a lighter vehicle, weighing about 8 cwt. in its original form, and its engine was at the rear. The cooling water circulated through the tubular chassis. The maximum speed provided by the $3\frac{1}{2}$-h.p. engine, turning at 600 r.p.m., was around 20 m.p.h. The prototype is said to have been fitted with the first radiator seen on a car, from an idea of Gaston Menier, the chocolate manufacturer who had bought one of Serpollet's steamers. Radiators were not a standard fitting as early as 1894, but surviving cars of around this age have since been fitted with gilled-tube radiators. This model was current until 1896, when a horizontal 8-h.p. engine of Peugeot manufacture, radiator cooled, replaced the Panhard unit. This car, capable of 26 m.p.h., was current until 1901, with a 5-h.p. version alongside it that would reach 15 m.p.h. Twenty-nine Peugeots were made in 1892, 40 in 1894, and 72 in 1895. By 1897 some 400 cars had been built.

10   BREMER, 1894, Great Britain

The Bremer is a competitor, with the Knight (12), for the title of Britain's first four-wheeled, internal-combustion-engined car. It still exists, in the Walthamstow Museum, London, and is in running order. The influence in the design of the Benz (6) from Germany is clear, even if the copy is more crudely executed—the Bremer was the first of a long line of British cars to follow that successful pattern. Its builder was a young engineer called Frederick W. Bremer, of Walthamstow, but the date of its completion is uncertain: 1894 is probable.

11 BERNARDI, 1894, Italy

Professor Enrico Bernardi built a gasoline engine in 1883, and eleven years later was responsible for Italy's first car. It was an original and advanced concept, as far as the engine was concerned. The little three-wheeler's power unit boasted a detachable cylinder-head, overhead valves, automatic lubrication, a jet carburettor of Maybach type, and fuel and air filters. It was capable of turning at 800 r.p.m., at which speed it developed up to $2\frac{1}{2}$ b.h.p. and drove the 6-cwt. car at 20 m.p.h. The S.A. Miari e Giusti of Padua acquired the Bernardi patents in 1896 and began to make his car under the name of Miari e Giusti. As was common at this early date, cars were built with minor variations, as illustrated. Notably, the machine above has wheel steering, while the one below is steered by tiller. In the same year, a four-wheeler was built. A model with a 3/5-h.p. engine was put into production in 1899. The firm went into liquidation in 1901, unable to compete with conventional small cars such as the F.I.A.T. (35), and French imports and derivations.

12 KNIGHT, 1895, Great Britain

The Knight, with the Bremer (10), was Britain's first internal-combustion-engined car, but the former was an original design. John Henry Knight of Farnham in Surrey had made a steam car as long ago as 1868. Later he turned to stationary oil (paraffin, kerosene) engines. A Knight oil engine powered the car shown, which still exists in running order in the Montagu Motor Museum at Beaulieu. It was built in the spring of 1895. For installation in a car, the oil engine was given a surface carburettor so that gasoline could be used. The vehicle was originally built as a three-wheeler, as seen in the upper illustration, but this layout, as usual, proved unstable, and in 1896 it was converted to a four-wheeler (lower illustration). Each front wheel is in a bicycle-type fork with its own coil spring, affording a form of independent front suspension. The car was capable of 8 m.p.h., and was used until 1898, when Knight became an enthusiast for the Benz from Germany (40).

13 PANHARD-LEVASSOR, 1895, France

The car illustrated was of the type which set the first fashion in automobile design. It became the norm for more expensive cars throughout the world, and then spread to all classes of vehicle. Its beginnings were as remote as 1879, when Edouard Sarazin became the French representative of Otto & Langen. Seven years later, he was Daimler's agent for France, controlling

French manufacturing rights in the Daimler engine. Emile Levassor, a maker (with René Panhard) of woodworking and metalworking machinery, built some engines for Sarazin to keep the latter's rights alive. Sarazin died in 1887, upon which his widow obtained the rights. She married Levassor, and made the rights over to him. Levassor's aim was to make a complete car, not just a carriage propelled by an engine. It first ran successfully in 1890, and was put on sale in 1891. After experiments with rear and centre location, Levassor finally placed the engine at the front of his car, in a box, in the interests of good weight distribution and adhesion for the steering road wheels. The power unit was a vee-twin of 1889 Daimler type, giving $3\frac{1}{2}$ b.h.p. at 600 r.p.m. Belt primary drive sometimes meant loss of power, which could hardly be spared in early cars, so Levassor devised the sliding-pinion gear-box, used in conjunction with a friction clutch and single-chain final drive. There were three forward speeds, all indirect, and the gears were exposed. Front engine position, sliding-pinion gear-box, rear-wheel drive—the fundamentals of the motor-car were there, only lately eroded by the recent spread of front-wheel drive and rear engines. The surface carburettors of the first cars were replaced by the Maybach-type jet carburettor in 1893. In that year Hippolyte Panhard, son of René, drove a Panhard-Levassor from Paris to Nice in eight days. Compared with the Benz and the Peugeot (40, 9), the only other gasoline passenger cars in the world to be in production, it was complicated and expensive. In 1895 a new type of Panhard won the world's first motor

race, from Paris to Bordeaux. It was powered by the much lighter, more efficient engine, with two vertical cylinders of the type pioneered by Daimler three years earlier, which in the Panhard developed 4 b.h.p. at 750–800 r.p.m. At the same time the gears were enclosed, and double-chain drive provided. Known as the 'Phoenix' in front-engined cars, this unit could propel the vehicle at $18\frac{1}{2}$ m.p.h. This Panhard, the type shown in the drawing, was put into production in 1896.

14 ROCHET-SCHNEIDER, 1895, France

Rochet-Schneider was a Lyons make that first appeared in 1894. Its earliest cars, of which two variations are illustrated, followed the Benz (6) school of thought, with their large, slow-running engines and electric ignition. They weighed 12 cwt., and were capable of around 20 m.p.h. The firm continued to make solid, conventional, worthy cars until 1932. They must have had something, since in their early days licences to build them were obtained by Nagant and F.N. in Belgium, by Florentia in Italy, and by Martini in Switzerland.

15 LANZA, 1895, 1898, Italy

Michele Lanza was an industrialist of Turin with a dilettante but deep faith in the future of the motor vehicle. Business trips took him to Paris, where he saw cars in use. The machine that he caused to be built in the little works of the Martina brothers in 1895 was the foundation stone of the vast Turin motor industry of today. It is difficult to realize that at that time, great technical difficulties were encountered by the Martinas, before the car was finished: even though the 8-h.p. engine was made under licence from a foreign manufacturer. A carriage-type body was fitted. In 1898 Lanza built a second car, much lighter and smaller, with a 5-h.p. engine but otherwise more advanced. This phaeton had equal-sized wheels front and rear, Ackermann steering, pneumatic tyres, a differential, and a three-speed gear-box. In the same year, the Fabbrica di Automobili Michele Lanza offered it to the public, with a choice of several body styles, but only seven cars in all were made up to 1903, for Lanza, like Siegfried Markus (2) was a perfectionist who would not stop experimenting and modifying; he would never standardize a model. Later, in the 1920s, he interested himself in aerodynamic bodywork for cars.

16 PENNINGTON
AUTOCAR, 1896,
Great Britain, U.S.A.

Misconceived mechanical inspiration was a commonplace in the early, exploratory days of the motor-car, and the Pennington is chosen here as an example, since no other device of such monstrous inefficiency was persisted with so tenaciously. Edward Joel Pennington of Chicago was a highly plausible company promoter of considerable vision and limited mechanical talent. A company he organized in Racine, Wisconsin in 1895 claimed to make cars using the Kane–Pennington Hot Air

Engine, Kane being the Chicago businessman who financed it. The cylinders were plain steel tubes, for Pennington's engine was supposed to cool itself by heat dissipation from the cylinder walls. There was no carburettor. Gasoline was fed direct into the induction pipe from the fuel tank by a valve: a form of fuel injection. The air and liquid gasoline mixture, drawn into the cylinder, was alleged to be first vaporized and then ignited by another Pennington peculiarity: the 'long-mingling spark'. This was allegedly provided by a heated wire spiral inside the cylinder. Though ingenious, Pennington's engines were very crude, with their exposed motion and tentative lubrication. Finally, Pennington did not believe in road springs, relying on pneumatic tyres of large section instead. Pennington's ideas worked badly, but just well enough to have his work published in respectable technical journals in an age of ignorance, and just well enough to support his gift of the gab. Four Penningtons were entered in the *Chicago Times–Herald* Race of 1895, but did not start. In 1896 Pennington went to Britain to promote his ideas. H. J. Lawson, busily attempting to gain control of the nascent British motor industry, bought his patents and established him in the Humber factory in Coventry to make his cars. The strange tricycle illustrated was one of the few vehicles that emerged. Even stranger is the fact that it still survives in complete form, in the Montagu Motor Museum at Beaulieu. Later Pennington machines had conventionally water-jacketed cylinders and normal ignition arrangements, but this did not save them. In 1899 Pennington floated the Anglo-American

Rapid Vehicle Company, a grandiose operation designed to take over some 200 patents and all existing British and American car designs. It collapsed, and its instigator fell into obscurity.

17 THOMSON, 1896, Australia

The Thomson Steam Phaeton was probably the first Australian-built automobile to run successfully. Its creator was Herbert Thomson, an engineer of Melbourne, Victoria. His machine ran at Armadale in that state in 1896, and in the same year it defeated a German Benz (40), Australia's first imported car, but the 1896 Thomson's most famous achievement was the nation's earliest long-distance, inter-state run by car, undertaken in 1900 between Bathurst in New South Wales and Melbourne. The distance of 493 miles was accomplished at an average speed of 8·72 m.p.h. Thomson made ten steam buggies of a slightly different design. His machines were practical and well-publicized enough to attract nearly 150 orders, and they were offered as catalogue models. However, Thomson soon found that he made a better living importing foreign cars, and dropped his steamers.

18 FORD, 1896, U.S.A.

Henry Ford, then chief engineer of the Edison Illuminating Company, built his first car in Detroit in 1896 and ran it in June of that year. It was a light, simple machine that he described as a quadricycle—a vehicle with as much in

common with a bicycle as with a car—rather than as an automobile. The impression was heightened by its wire wheels and pneumatic tyres. The first Ford was a conservative design, with its exposed crankshaft, flywheel and connecting rods, belt drive throughout, and lack of a differential, but weighing only $4\frac{1}{2}$ cwt., it could attain 25 m.p.h. with an engine developing 3 b.h.p. at 600 r.p.m. Only one of these cars was made. Not until 1899 could Ford get financial backing for his first venture into car manufacture, the Detroit Automobile Company (88).

19 KING, 1896, U.S.A.

Charles Brady King, an engineer of Detroit, saw a two-stroke gasoline engine made by the Sintz Gas Engine Company at the Chicago World's Fair of 1893, and ordered one. Later in the same year, he designed a motor tricycle, and in 1893-4, designed two four-wheeled cars. During 1895 he built a four-stroke, four-cylinder engine, and entered a car with such an engine in the *Chicago Times–Herald* Race of that year. It did not appear; the first King car to take the road did so in March of 1896. It was still the first working automobile to be made in Detroit, beating the Ford by about three months, and was one of the first in the world to have a four-cylinder in-line engine. This unit developed some 3 b.h.p., which propelled the 12-cwt. car at between 7 and 8 m.p.h. in the streets of Detroit. The body was made by the Emerson & Fisher Carriage Company, which had been trying to create interest in the new form of locomotion. Both they and

King were ahead of their time. King's comment, that motor-cars were 'much in vogue among the English aristocracy and will undoubtedly soon be here', was an understatement in the classic mould. He had, indeed, started something. Although he made no more cars for some years, he continued to play a part in the new industry. King supplied Henry Ford with valves, then later worked for Oldsmobile (74) and Northern. He made his own car again from 1910 until 1924.

20 VABIS, 1897, Sweden

The Vagnfabriks A.B. i. Sodertalje were assemblers of railroad wagons for the Surahammar iron and steelworks, makers of rolling-stock parts. In 1897 Gustav Erikson, an engineer at Surahammar who had studied automobile design in France and Britain, built his employers an engine for use in road vehicles. It was an extremely original design. Erikson was against gasoline as a fuel. He made an engine with four cylinders in vee formation. In a separate combustion chamber, air was heated by a paraffin (kerosene) burner and compressed, then injected into the cylinders. This engine, which was designed to produce 6 b.h.p. and to power a motor vehicle, failed. Another, a four-stroke unit with two horizontal cylinders, and a governor by which the fuel/air ratio was automatically adjusted to suit the load, was built and mounted in the rear of a wagon supplied by C. A. Carlson & Sons of Stockholm. This is the vehicle illustrated, which is in Stockholm's Tekniska Museet. It did not run well,

and collided with a wall. At one stage in its life, it was fitted with skis (lower illustration) for winter use. A third engine with hot-tube ignition was also a failure; and now Erikson admitted defeat, abandoned his paraffin engines, and fitted the car with a conventional vee-twin gasoline unit. The Vagnfabriks A.B. made occasional cars up to 1907, when it was reorganized to concentrate on motor vehicles, most of them trucks (which had been built since 1903). Four years later, in 1911, came amalgamation with the Maskin A.B. Scania (59) to form A.B. Scania-Vabis.

21 VALLÉE, 1897, France

The Vallée was built at Le Mans between 1896 and 1901, the model illustrated being current from 1897 to 1899, with variations in bodywork and detail as shown. In its design there was much of the Benz from Germany (40)—belt primary drive, steering-column gearchange, etc.—and in this the Vallée followed a popular trend. The model illustrated is a *vis-à-vis*; that is to say, with facing seats. The vehicle illustrated above is in the Musée National de l'Automobile, Rochetaillée-sur-Saône.

22 MENON, 1897, Italy

Carlo Menon's firm, founded in 1875, built a few cars at Roncade de Treviso between 1897 and 1902. The $3\frac{1}{2}$-h.p. engine was conventional enough except for the fact that it was designed to run on an alcohol/gasoline mixture, but the transmission was not. A drum on the rear axle was driven positively by belt. Changes of speed were effected not by pulleys, as was usual with belt drive; for inside the drum was a single reduction gear. Maximum speed was a respectable 25 m.p.h. or so.

23 LANCHESTER, 1897-8, Great Britain

Frederick William Lanchester had one of the most original minds in the pioneer motor industry, but he came to automobile manufacture by default. The works manager of a gas engine firm, he occupied himself with the theory of aerial flight. By 1893 he had come to the conclusion that a flying machine would need a far lighter engine than any then existing, and he was dissuaded from pursuing this line by the remoteness of its possibilities. Instead, he turned to the nearer prospect of the motor-car. In the same year Lanchester made a gasoline engine that ran successfully in a boat for many years. He studied French and German cars, saw that they were all derived in one way or another from stationary engine, bicycle or horse-carriage principles, and decided to design a car from scratch. The result, which was on the road in 1896, was a completely new concept. With its live axle, direct drive on top gear, mechanically-operated inlet valve, low-tension magneto ignition, and self-centering lever steering, it was well ahead of its time. There was a single-cylinder, 5-h.p. air-cooled engine. It was centrally located, and drove to an epicyclic gear-box. There was chain final drive. The car was underpowered, so in 1897 it was given an

8-h.p. flat-twin engine, mounted at the rear. The final drive was now by worm gears, and on this car only, experiments were carried out with a raked steering wheel. These features were novelties. A second car, that illustrated (and kept in the Science Museum, London), was built in 1897 and was running in the following year. At different times in its career, it wore the differing bodies and wings illustrated. This two-passenger phaeton had the 8-h.p. engine, rear-mounted. For its day, it was an extraordinarily smooth-running unit, thanks to its twin crankshafts and flywheels rotating in opposite directions, and other care paid to balance. The quite considerable power output of a large engine was developed at the high speed of 1200 r.p.m., snd enabled this car to reach 30 m.p.h. One journey of sixty-eight miles was covered at an average speed of 28 m.p.h. This was a very high average for a passenger car in 1898. One replica with a four-passenger body was made, but until late 1900 no other Lanchesters were constructed. The Lanchester Engine Company was launched in 1899 to market motor-cars.

24 STEPHENS, 1898, Great Britain

Richard Stephens of Clevedon in Somerset was a bicycle maker and general engineer who devised a much refined and more sophisticated version of the Benz (40). It was an improvement on its contemporary from Germany by virtue of its engine, which was considerably bigger, and gave a better power-to-weight ratio, providing around 10 b.h.p. at 800 r.p.m. for a weight of 11 cwt. The motor also had more efficient water cooling. Maximum speed was 25 m.p.h. Front suspension was independent, a very advanced feature, with each wheel in a separate fork, and a single transverse spring. Stephens' first car is illustrated. Few were built. Stephens also made some six- and nine-passenger types for public service work. A six-passenger version was the first motor taxi to appear in the city of Bath. These larger cars differed from the private passenger cars by having larger engines, jet carburettors, and hot-tube ignition.

25 DECAUVILLE, 1898, France

Joseph Guédon sold his design for a small car to the Société Decauville, locomotive manufacturers of Corbeil, in 1897, who gave it the attractive name *voiturelle*, with its avian connotations, because the term *voitur. tte* was already in use by Léon Bollée (29). The Decauville *voiturelle* was made from 1898 to 1901. It was an assembled car, taking advantage of De Dion (32) components, like an increasing number of its contemporaries. The engine consisted of two De Dion-type $1\frac{1}{4}$-h.p. tricycle units in tandem, sharing a single crankcase casting. The ignition, too, was of De Dion-type. This power unit developed some 3 b.h.p. at 1200 r.p.m., providing 30 m.p.h., at the cost of noise that was noticeable even in an age when mechanical din was tolerated in motor-cars. There was independent front wheel suspension by sliding pillars and a transverse spring; one of the earliest known applications

of independent suspension to a production car. In spite of its failings, the *voiturelle* gained a reputation for reliability and manoeuvrability. It was a little slower than the Léon Bollée, its rival, but won its class in the Paris–Amsterdam Race of 1898 and the Tour de France of 1899, among other successes. The *voiturelle* was made in Germany by Ehrhardt at Eisenach as the Wartburgwagen (81), and in Italy as the Marchand (80). It was replaced by a more conventional machine in 1901, which had a water-cooled engine at the front and three forward speeds.

26 POPP, 1898, Switzerland

Lorenz Popp was an engineer of Basle who, with the financial aid of Edouard Burkhardt, the Swiss agent for Benz (40), made two cars of Benz derivation in 1898. The engine was original, in that the valves were operated by a single chain-driven overhead camshaft. It developed around 7 b.h.p. One of the two cars Popp made still exists, in the Verkehrshaus der Schweiz in Lucerne. Later, Popp became the agent in Zurich for the German Stoewer (29) and the Italian F.I.A.T. cars (35).

27 ORIENT EXPRESS, 1898, Germany

In 1895 Bergmann's Industriewerke of Gaggenau, who also made bicycles, started to build a car on Benz lines (40), which they called by the very un-German name of Orient Express, presumably because it sold best in England and France. Its designer was the engineer Joseph Vollmer. The original engine developed between 3 and 4 b.h.p., being replaced in 1900 by a slightly larger unit of 6 b.h.p. It was notable for its use of Simms-Bosch-type low-tension magneto ignition; the Orient Express was one of the first production cars to be so equipped. Some cars may have had friction drive, but most used belt-and-chain drive as did the Benz. It is possible, in fact, that the last few cars made had Benz engines. It was an Orient Express that was the 'villain' of that classic early motoring novel, *The Lightning Conductor* by C. N. and A. M. Williamson. It was a make with a bad reputation for unreliability, which is surprising considering its solidly respectable derivation. The company was taken over by Benz in 1907.

28 GRÄF, 1898, Austria

Karl, Franz, and Heinrich Gräf were bicycle repairers who between 1895 and 1897 put together the little car illustrated, which was the only one made and first ran in 1898. It is in the Technisches Museum für Industrie und Gewerbe in Vienna. A De Dion-Bouton engine, of the type that was sold to numerous makers of assembled vehicles, was installed above the front axle and drove the wheels by shafts separate from the axle, in the approved De Dion manner (32). It developed its power at 1500 r.p.m. The gear-box, however, was made by Karl Gräf. After Willy Stift joined the firm, the manufacture of small cars continued, the name Gräf und Stift being introduced in 1902. These cars still had French engines, but made by Buchet and

Mutel. The company also built a car called the Spitz to the order of Arnold Spitz, Austria's largest car dealer.

29 STOEWER, 1899, Germany

In 1858 Bernhard Stoewer set up a small firm in Stettin to make sewing-machines, and later typewriters and bicycles. His sons Bernhard junior and Emil went into motor-cycle and tricycle manufacture in 1897, winning medals for them at the Berlin Motor Show of 1899. The tricycle was of De Dion type, powered by a Cudell engine, which was a De Dion-Bouton unit made under licence in Germany. A quadricycle arrived in the same year of 1899, still powered by a single-cylinder Cudell engine, and with it a full-scale car; that illustrated. In 1901 the company went over to the Panhard-Levassor system with a four-cylinder, front-engined car, and other two- and four-cylinder types followed.

30 DAIMLER, 1899, Germany

The vehicle illustrated, in the Montagu Motor Museum, is a representative of the Daimler Motoren Gesellschaft's first serious run of production cars, which began in 1895. The model was current until 1900, but was basically similar to the very first Daimler car of 1886 (4). The main improvements were the two-cylinder vertical in-line engine and its Maybach jet carburettor. There was nothing here of the intermediate, precocious 'Steel Wheel Car' of 1889 (see 4), and nothing of Emile Levassor's very modern Panhard-Levassor, also in production. The reason for such conservatism was that the original design, as subsequently modified, was simple, strong, reliable, easy to control, and quiet in operation, even if slow and behind the times. No other car of the 1890s could offer this combination of virtues, except the Benz (40) and its derivatives. The engine developed $4\frac{1}{2}$ b.h.p. at a governed speed of 750 r.p.m., which gave the car a maximum speed of around 16 m.p.h. This was about as much as the centre-pivot steering would tolerate. Other sizes of engine could be fitted, providing between 2 and 6 b.h.p., and so could other bodies, with room for 2, 4, or 6 passengers. During the currency of this model, a more modern type of Daimler had already been introduced that was on the lines of the successful Panhard-Levassor of 1895-6. This Phoenix-type Daimler had a front engine, a clutch, and a four-speed sliding-pinion gear-box instead of belts, and chain final drive. In 1898 it improved upon the Panhard by adopting Simms-Bosch low-tension magneto ignition.

31 LÉON BOLLÉE, 1899,
France

The Bollée family of Le Mans were at first more closely associated with steam vehicles than gasoline cars. Amedée Bollée the younger, son of Amedée Bollée senior, creator of a famous line of steam carriages, in 1887 built a single-cylinder four-stroke gasoline engine, followed by a three-cylinder rotary unit, and a two-stroke. His brother Léon, a skilled engineer who had already devised a calculating machine,

designed the family's first gasoline car in 1895. It was a three-wheeler that first appeared in May 1896. Léon's aims were light weight and a low centre of gravity, and simplicity of construction. He hoped thus to obtain performance coupled with reliability and stability; the last in spite of the Léon Bollée being a tricar. This was a combination conspicuously lacking in contemporary Benzes and Daimlers and their derivatives. Bollée called his curious tandem two-seater a *voiturette*; a name which was at first applied to his cars only. With an engine developing $2\frac{1}{2}$ b.h.p. at a governed speed of 700-800 r.p.m., but capable of the very high speed of 1200 r.p.m., in a vehicle weighing only $3\frac{1}{4}$ cwt., he certainly achieved performance to the tune of 30 m.p.h. and more, but the simplicity of the design was translated as crudity, which did not help make for dependability. The gearing was direct on the crankshaft, in mesh with other gears on a layshaft; a clutch action being obtained by fore-and-aft movement, by means of a lever, of the single rear wheel, this controlling the tension of the belt. The cylinder-head was uncooled and therefore liable to overheating. Primitive features such as these did not prevent the Léon Bollée's superior speed winning its class and making the fastest times of *any* car in the Paris–Dieppe and Paris–Trouville races of 1897. In the latter event it averaged 28·2 m.p.h., 3 m.p.h. faster than the best Panhard-Levassor (13). H. J. Lawson bought the patents, but his manufacturing plans were delayed by a fire. The car was subsequently built as the Coventry Motette, with certain improvements such as a cylinder-head finned for cooling. The

Léon Bollée was made until 1899, when it was superseded by a 9-h.p. four-wheeler with semi-independent front suspension. A line of conventional luxury cars followed in 1903.

32 DE DION-BOUTON,
1899, France

Although he began by making light passenger steamers (3), the Comte de Dion had been concerning himself with gasoline engine developments since 1889, and in four years work had begun on a prototype gasoline vehicle, though commercial and public service steamers continued to be made until 1899. His designer Georges Bouton developed a tiny, high-speed, lightweight engine weighing only 66 lb. but capable of turning at upwards of 1500 r.p.m. continuously without shaking itself to pieces. This, in larger form, was fitted to a motor-tricycle that took the road in 1895, and when put into production, the tricycle proved very popular. The first motor-cars were put on sale in 1899. A few, in 1900, had $2\frac{3}{4}$-h.p. engines of 326 c.c., with detachable water-cooled cylinder-head and air-cooled cylinder-barrel, but a $3\frac{1}{2}$-h.p. unit, fully water-cooled, was standardized. In 1901 the final development of the rear-engined car had a $4\frac{1}{2}$-h.p. engine of 500 c.c., a lever replaced the wheel used hitherto for changing gear, and for the first time a reverse gear was supplied. The most enduring feature of the first De Dion-Bouton car was its live rear axle design. Evolved in principle by Trépardoux for his steamers, it consisted of a final drive and differential assembly mounted on the chassis frame,

therefore forming part of the sprung weight of the car, driving by universally-jointed shafts to the rear wheels, which were attached to the extremities of a dead axle that ran behind the drive shafts. This system allowed the axle to move in relation to the frame while avoiding the necessity for chain drive to this end. These little cars were so popular that they can be said to have established the practical small car. The contemporary Benz design (40) was solid and reliable enough, but the power-to-weight ratio of the latter's engine, and consequently the car's performance, did not compare with those of the De Dion-Bouton, which was utterly dependable and easy to control into the bargain. A London dealership was established in the first months of production. About 1500 examples had been sold everywhere by April 1901, and production was said to be running at the (then) fabulous rate of 200 cars a month by the end of the year. The engines alone were even more sought-after. By the middle of 1903, 40,000 had been sold, some with bespoke cylinder dimensions, to more than 100 other car constructors. Some versions, such as the Pierce Motorette in America, were in fact De Dions in every respect. However, in 1902 rear-engined cars were out of fashion, and production was turned over by degrees to front-engined machines. At the same time, bigger engines of 6 and 8 h.p. (700 and 864 c.c.) became available. The best-received De Dion of all was the 6 h.p. in Populaire (two-passenger) form, which, weighing only 6 cwt., was capable of nearly 30 m.p.h. The 8-h.p. model acquired three forward speeds late in 1902, and was in production for another five years. Later in 1905, a new type of single-cylinder De Dion made its appearance, with pressed-steel instead of tubular chassis, a mechanical inlet valve, a radiator raised to a normal level from its previous underhung position, and a normal sliding-pinion gearbox. In 1911 the last characteristic of the first cars, the De Dion axle, was abandoned, and a year later the single-cylinder engine finally disappeared.

33 GOBRON-BRILLIÉ, 1899, France

In 1898 Gustave Gobron and Eugène Brillié of the Société Gobron-Brillié of Boulogne-sur-Seine started to make cars with engines of remarkable design. They were opposed-piston units, each cylinder containing two pistons. Two of the four pistons were attached direct to the crankshaft, and the other two were linked to it by crossheads and connecting rods. The crankshaft was balanced, and the engine was rubber-mounted. These features together were intended to provide great smoothness of running, and did so. There were originally two forward speeds, later increased to three. The 6-h.p. engine was mounted at the rear, as in the car illustrated, but then, in 1901, migrated to the front in response to current fashion. The indicated horsepower was produced at 1000 r.p.m., driving the one-ton car at around 26 m.p.h. Brillié's design met with no great success, being too unconventional, and later cars of the 1920s used normal, proprietary engines supplied by Chapuis-Dornier. The Gobron-Brillié's main claim to fame was as the world's first gasoline car to exceed 100 m.p.h., in 1904. This was a special four-cylinder racing machine built the previous year. The car shown is displayed in the Musée National de l'Automobile, Rochetaillée-sur-Saône.

34 PRINETTI & STUCCHI, 1899, Italy

In its first incarnation, the Prinetti & Stucchi was a simple quadricycle with a single-cylinder, 258-c.c. engine, giving $1\frac{3}{4}$ h.p. It was succeeded by a small car proper, of which one is illustrated. It exists in the Museo dell' Automobile in Turin. Its power unit had two cylinders of the same dimensions, providing around 4 b.h.p. at the high speed of 1500 r.p.m. The weight was less than 5 cwt. Ettore Bugatti is said to have contributed to the development of these cars.

35 F.I.A.T., 1899, Italy

In 1899, Giovanni Agnelli, Count Biscaretti di Ruffia and Count Bricherasio founded the Fabbrica Italiana di Automobili in Turin, taking the initials of the firm's name and the initial of the city as the car's name. Not until 1906 were the full points dropped altogether. To acquire knowhow, F.I.A.T. first acquired the Welleyes car design made by Giovanni Ceirano's bicycle manufacturing concern of that name. The Welleyes used a De Dion-Bouton engine (32), and was designed by Aristide Faccioli. The latter now designed the first F.I.A.T. car, of which ten had been made by November 1899.

The engine, rated at $3\frac{1}{2}$ h.p., in fact developed over 4 b.h.p., at the low engine speed of 400 r.p.m. The weight of the complete car was rather over 13 cwt. A 6-h.p. and 8-h.p. model followed in 1900. Fifty of these were built that year. A completely new type of F.I.A.T., based on the German Mercedes design (60), arrived in 1902, though the 8-h.p. twin was sold into the same year.

36 DANSK AUTOMOBIL OG CYKEL FABRIK H. C. CHRISTIANSEN, about 1899, Denmark

With the Hammel (5), this little machine is one of Denmark's two oldest known surviving automobiles. The Copenhagen firm that made it, H. C. Christiansen & Company, went on to provide the capital with its first motor taxis in 1904, and built cars until 1906. Before being identified, the vehicle illustrated was thought to be an imported French car, since it has a Longuemare carburettor and shares other characteristics of French light cars of the time. The 3-h.p. engine was made by the manufacturers. The car, which is more briefly known as the Dansk or Christiansen, still exists, in the care of the Danish Technical Museum.

37 LOCOMOBILE, 1900, U.S.A.

In 1897 Francis E. Stanley of Newton, Massachusetts, the maker of such variegated products as musical instruments, gas generators, and photographic equipment, built a light steam car. A few

were sold, but in 1899 Francis, who had by now been joined by his brother Freelan O., disposed of the design to A. L. Barber and Brisbane Walker of the Locomobile Company of America, who proceeded to sell the little car with great success. The Locomobile was the first (and the only) popular steam car, owing its favourable reception to its great simplicity and ease of control, as compared with most gasoline cars. The complete vehicle weighed only 7 cwt. However, it was frail, and its range was limited by its water capacity of twenty miles and the gasoline supply for the generator, which was good for ten miles. It was, in fact, a town runabout, not practical, versatile transportation. Two slightly differing versions are shown. The car above has a box in front of the dashboard, wings, and side-lever steering; the lower car has tiller steering and no wings. The Locomobile was made from 1900 to 1904, but already, in 1903, its makers had started to build gasoline cars. Meanwhile the Stanley brothers, enabled by their agreement with Locomobile to restart motor manufacture in 1902, had gone on to offer an entirely different design of steamer. The factory continued to build steam cars exclusively until the middle 1920s.

38 NESSELSDORF, 1900, Austria

The Nesselsdorfer Wagenbau Fabrik Gesselschaft started life as a cart and carriage manufacturing business in the town of Nesselsdorf (now Koprovnice) in Moravia, then went on to railroad rolling-stock. An experimental car, called the President, was built in 1897 with a 5-h.p. Benz engine (40) that gave a top speed of about 15 m.p.h. In the following year, manufacture was started with a similar car powered by a 9-h.p. Benz engine providing 20 m.p.h. but furnished with Simms-Bosch low-tension magneto ignition; a very modern feature. The gear-box was designed by Hans Ledwinka, later to be famous for his designs for the successor of the Nesselsdorf, the Tatra; and for Steyr. One of this model, of which ten were made in all, is illustrated. Racing versions were built, with 12- and 18-h.p. engines turning over at 1800 r.p.m., that could allegedly reach 70 m.p.h.

39 LOHNER-PORSCHE, 1900, Austria

Jacob Lohner & Company were carriage builders and makers of electrical equipment. They were persuaded to unite the two activities by the young Ferdinand Porsche, who after his apprenticeship, joined the firm in 1896. The electric cars illustrated are a brougham (top) and a Victoria. The motors were in the front hubs. The armature of each was fastened to a hub, and the stationary field was fastened to the axle; therefore the rate of wheel rotation was the same as the motor speed. Each motor was of $2\frac{1}{2}$ nominal h.p., but could be boosted to 7 h.p. Without the heavy batteries, the brougham weighed 15 cwt. The range imposed on these vehicles by battery life between charges was twenty miles, which meant that, like all its kind, the Lohner-Porsche was restricted to pottering in a dignified fashion about town. However, the design must have had something, since by 1902 thirty-five manufacturers had taken out Lohner-Porsche licences. Porsche also designed 'mixed' or petrol-electric vehicles for Lohner in which a gasoline engine drove a generator which provided power to the motors in the front wheel hubs. An experimental petrol-electric Austro-Daimler by Porsche followed in the 1920s.

40 BENZ, 1900, Germany

The Benz Victoria of 1893 (see 6), the first production gasoline-engined car, was developed into the *vis-à-vis* model of 1894, with different seating arrangements. Both were big cars, with options of engines giving up to $5\frac{1}{2}$ b.h.p. Alongside them there appeared a much smaller machine (though one still based on the Victoria), that was the world's earliest attempt to produce a cheap car for a popular market. This was the Velo. At first its engine was said to develop $1\frac{1}{2}$ b.h.p. at 500 r.p.m.; later this was increased to $2\frac{3}{4}$ b.h.p., and then (as in the car illustrated) to $3-3\frac{1}{2}$ b.h.p. at 750–800 r.p.m. (although the engine dimensions did not change). The maximum speed rose at the same time from 12 m.p.h. to around 17 m.p.h. Cruising speed was around 14 m.p.h. From 1897 the Velo's bigger brethren could also be had with horizontally-opposed twin-cylinder engines in various sizes. The first major change affecting all types came in 1898, when the original two forward speeds, already with their own belts and levers, were supplemented on all Benz models by a Crypto epicyclic emergency low gear, controlled by a third lever. With the Crypto, the Benz could climb any but the most abnormal hills, given time. An improved Velo was offered as the Comfortable, an addition justified by two extra, very small seats facing the driver and the option of pneumatic tyres. The whole car weighed 8 cwt. One of these, and also a normal Velo, which was still listed, are shown. Engine power was creeping up, so cooling was improved in 1898–9 by fitting a gilled-tube radiator and a water-pump on all models except the Velo. At the same time, low-tension magneto ignition was available on the bigger cars. These larger models were also provided with a reverse gear. By now they included the luxurious Mylord coupé and the eight-passenger Break. The last development of the Velo was the Ideal, still with engine at the rear, though on some cars a dummy hood followed fashion. It was current from about 1900 to 1902, and could be had in $3\frac{1}{2}$-h.p. or $4\frac{1}{2}$-h.p. form. The simplicity, reliability, ease of control, longevity, and low running costs of the Benz made it the first car to become something more than a rich man's toy; the first approach to a 'popular' car. From its introduction the cheap, light Velo was the Benz with the widest appeal. Its price was less than half that of the Panhard-Levassor. Of 134 Benzes built in 1895, 62 were Velos, 36 were Victorias, and 20 were *vis-à-vis*. By the end of another three years 200 Benzes had been sold in Britain and another 200 in France. In 1899 572 cars were sold. By the end of that year the grand total was 2000. In 1900, the peak year, 603 cars found customers. By this time, the design was obsolete; the up-to-date small car was exemplified by

the De Dion (32) and the Renault (54). It was not surprising that only 265 Ideals, the final variation on the original Benz theme, were sold. In 1903 a completely revised and modernized range of cars appeared (92, 93).

41 **ADLER,** 1900, Germany

Heinrich Kleyer of Frankfurt started making bicycles in 1886, then added typewriters to his products. He fitted engines to his bicycles, and in 1899 built an experimental motor-car, which was put into production in the following year. He followed the Renault system (54), powering his car with a front-mounted De Dion-Bouton engine (32) of $3\frac{1}{2}$ h.p., and coupling it with Renault transmission—via a cone clutch, sliding-pinion gear-box, and shaft drive to a live rear axle. This little car, which was made from 1900 to 1903, and is illustrated here, weighed under 8 cwt. and could reach 20 m.p.h. The Adler was developed as more powerful De Dion single-cylinder engines became available, a $4\frac{1}{2}$-h.p. model appearing in 1901 and a 6 h.p. and 8 h.p. in 1902. The last-named was good for 25 m.p.h. In 1903 Edmund Rumpler joined the firm, and instituted a new range of types of larger, two- and four-cylinder cars. He also produced an experimental Adler with unit construction of engine and gear-box, and swing-axle independent suspension.

42 **VIVINUS,** 1900, Belgium

Alexis Vivinus in 1899 introduced a successful small car that was current until 1901. Its engine developed $3\frac{1}{2}$ b.h.p. at 900 r.p.m., which sufficed to propel the vehicle, which weighed only $3\frac{1}{2}$ cwt., at 16 m.p.h. In 1900 there arrived alongside it a much faster (35 m.p.h.) Vivinus, which was updated in the following year. This used a water-cooled, vertical-twin cylinder engine producing 7 h.p., a three-speed sliding-pinion gear-box, and shaft drive, in the approved modern idiom. A new single-cylinder car, with water-cooled De Dion-Bouton engine (32) seems to have been introduced to replace the old single, which had by now been dropped. The latter was popular, being made as the New Orleans in Britain (one of these is illustrated here), as the Georges Richard (66) in France, and by De Dietrich (69) in Germany. In 1902 the Vivinus became a bigger car altogether, with the coming of a four-cylinder model with mechanically-operated inlet valves.

43 ARGYLL, 1900,
Great Britain

In 1896 Alexander Govan, a Scottish engineer, was working for the Scottish Cycle Manufacturing Company of Hozier Street, Glasgow. From these premises he sold, and later assembled Renault (54), De Dion-Bouton (32), and Darracq (55). Govan built his own first, prototype car in 1899, and in the following year the Hozier Engineering Company was founded to make cars seriously, to Govan's design. The first run, of about 100 vehicles, were clearly of Renault derivation, with their front engines driving by cone clutch, sliding-pinion gear-box, and shaft drive to a

live rear axle. Govan's gear-box, of his own design, was noted for being extremely difficult to operate, even in an age when sliding-pinion gear-boxes were the reverse of refined. It called for combined fore-and-aft and sideways movements of the lever. The first ninety or so cars had handle-bar steering, and $2\frac{3}{4}$-h.p. engines of 326 c.c. bought from the Motor Manufacturing Company, who built them under licence from De Dion-Bouton. Only the cylinder-head was cooled. The car illustrated, which is preserved by the Department of Technology of the Glasgow Art Gallery and Museum, has the later, larger, 5-h.p. M.M.C. engine, fully water-cooled, and wheel steering.

44 NAPIER, 1900,
Great Britain

In 1898 Montague Stanley Napier was at the head of D. Napier & Son, a small manufacturer of tools for the bicycle trade and coin-making machinery that had seen much better days. He was building an experimental car when an old friend, Selwyn Francis Edge, brought him his 1896 Panhard-Levassor (13) and asked him to convert it to the wheel steering that the great French make had just acquired. Edge, an Australian, had competed with Napier in their joint interest, cycle racing. In 1899 Edge came back to D. Napier & Son and asked them to fit a new, somewhat modified engine. Late in the same year, the two men made an agreement by which Napier would build his own cars and Edge, with capital provided by the financier Harvey du Cros, would run an almost independent selling organization, the Motor Power Company, which at first sold other makes of car as well as the Napier. The partnership's first cars, one of which is illustrated, appeared in 1900. This 8-h.p. model continued into 1901. Also in 1900, the company made its first four-cylinder car. This very advanced design had a four-cylinder engine cast mono-bloc in aluminium with iron liners, and three automatic inlet valves per cylinder. This car was entered, albeit unsuccessfully, in that year's Paris-Toulouse Race. A four-cylinder 24-h.p. car was in production by 1901, by which time commercial vehicles and dirigible balloons were also being offered. Edge made Napier's name by winning the 1902 Gordon Bennett Race, and the world's first series-production six-cylinder car came out of the factory in 1904 (95).

45 ENGLISH MECHANIC,
1900, Great Britain

Around the turn of the century, the journal *The English Mechanic and World of Science and Art* published a series of articles by a consulting engineer, T. Hyler-White, to show its readers how to make their own automobile. The home-built motor-car is no new thing, and was not confined to Britain; there were several in the U.S.A., including the Metz. *The English Mechanic* naturally used simple, tested, and accepted designs. One, that illustrated, was based on the Benz (40). Parts that the average amateur engineer could not make at home could be bought out, but this was no kit-car: full instructions for making engines, etc., were provided, and

addresses where, failing this, parts might be obtained—but nothing else. An engine of Benz type, though not identical, giving 3 h.p. at 700 r.p.m., was mated with Benz transmission. A speed of 14 m.p.h. was obtainable. Later, vertical single and twin-cylinder designs were added, and a steam car.

46 ROYAL ENFIELD QUAD,
1901, Great Britain

The Enfield Cycle Company, well-known bicycle manufacturers, started to make motor-tricycles and quadri-cycles at their Redditch, Worcestershire, factory in 1899. The quadri-cycles, one of which is illustrated, were powered by De Dion-Bouton (30) engines, like so many other light cars. They were fitted with either the $2\frac{3}{4}$-h.p. 326-c.c. or the $3\frac{1}{2}$-h.p. 402-c.c. unit, the former with a water-cooled cylinder-head only, and the latter fully water-cooled. Pedals were also provided, for extra assistance on hills. This type of machine was popular in Britain and Europe until the coming of the cycle-car, the first true motor-car in miniature, around 1910. In 1901 Enfield offered a more normal automobile, with a 6-h.p. vee-twin Ader (70) engine.

47 ALLDAYS TRAVELLER,
1901, Great Britain

The Birmingham engineering firm of Alldays & Onions had been founded as early as 1650, and were best known as makers of pneumatic machinery. Their first vehicle was a tricar, followed by a quadricycle, which developed into the much-improved Traveller Sociable Voiturette. This, in 1900, was the company's earliest production car. It was a four-wheeler, powered by a De Dion-Bouton engine (30) of $2\frac{3}{4}$ h.p. From 1902 an engine of Alldays' own manufacture was apparently used. An unexpected touch of sophistication so early in a machine of this type was the provision of wheel steering. As an alternative to a seat between the front wheels, a box for commercial travellers' samples could be substituted. The rear axle was unsprung; a common feature in light vehicles of the time. A reverse gear was provided for 1903. In the following year, the Traveller was joined by a car proper, with front $6\frac{1}{2}$-h.p. engine, the A1 type, and soon thereafter dropped.

48 SUNBEAM MABLEY,
1901, Great Britain

This machine, possibly the oddest produced by any motor manufacturer in the world at a time when anything went, was the product of a sober and extremely successful bicycle manufacturer of Wolverhampton, Staffordshire: John Marston. The contrast reflects the combination of ignorance, enthusiasm, and far-sightedness that characterized the industry in its earliest days. In fact Marston's first Sunbeam cars, of 1899, designed by Thomas Cureton, were much more conventional beasts with vertical or horizontal front engines and belt drive. However, they got no further than the experimental stage, and the first Sunbeam to be put into production was the outrageous vehicle illustrated. Designed

by a Mr Mabberley-Smith, its most obvious peculiarity was its wheel arrangement. They were in a diamond layout, but each had a different track, the front and rear wheels being out of line. These were the steering road wheels, and both turned together. The side wheels were the driving wheels. The object of the layout was to avoid skidding, one of the greatest dangers besetting the early motorist. Its success or failure is not recorded. The driver sat at the rear, with, in front of him and to one side, seated lengthwise, his two passengers. The power unit was the familiar single-cylinder De Dion unit of $2\frac{3}{4}$ h.p. Between 1901 and 1904 no fewer than 300 of this remarkable contrivance were sold. Its appeal was diminishing when T. C. Pullinger joined Marston and a separate company was set up to make cars. Pullinger's first machine, of 1902, was derived from the French Berliet, and was entirely normal.

49 ALBION, 1901,
Great Britain

George Johnston, who in 1895 owned one of the first cars imported into Scotland, was responsible for the first Scottish-built motor vehicle, made in the same year. Johnston, Sir William Arrol, T. Blackwood-Murray, and Norman Osborne Fulton formed the Mo-Car Syndicate and began to make cars under the name Arrol-Johnston (50). In 1899 Murray and Fulton broke away to make experimental cars of their own, and then to found the Albion Motor Car Company in Finnieston, Glasgow. Their first, the model

A1 Albion of 1901, had an 8-h.p. engine turning at 700 r.p.m., two forward speeds, and a close resemblance to the Arrol-Johnston; with which it shared Murray's low-tension chain-driven magneto ignition. This feature was seen in all two-cylinder Albions until 1914. The Albion was, however, an even simpler and much lighter design than the Arrol-Johnston. Twenty-one of these cars were built in 1901. The model A2, as illustrated, with three forward speeds, was made with the A1 until 1903. One hundred and fifty-nine of both types were built. Solidity and simplicity were the characteristics of the Albion; it was designed to last for ever on Scottish roads. Weight was $18\frac{1}{4}$ cwt. Modernity, at first, was a secondary consideration. Late in 1902, wheel steering was introduced with a bigger engine of 10 h.p., but the former was merely an optional extra at first. The A3 Albion of 1903, with a vertical engine of 12 h.p., of the same crudity but at the front, driving now by a separate chain to each rear wheel, was (outwardly at least) more up to date, and was current for eleven years. It was supplemented by the 16 h.p. (once again the same design, with enlarged bores). The two-cylinder engine was also used on the company's famous commercial vehicles, the first of which was offered in 1902 on the A2 chassis. A four-cylinder, 24-h.p. engine was introduced in 1906 for a luxury passenger car.

50 ARROL-JOHNSTON,
1901, Great Britain

Late in 1895 Sir William Arrol, George

Johnston, T. Blackwood-Murray, and Norman Osborne Fulton formed the Mo-Car Syndicate for the purpose of building the Arrol-Johnston motor-car, in that concern's factory at Cam-lachie. Murray and Fulton broke away in 1899 to make the Albion (49), which was on broadly similar but lighter and even simpler lines. The first few Arrol-Johnstons, of 1899–1900, had one cylinder only, and tiller steering. From 1901 they went over to two cylinders, and wheel steering. The engine was an opposed-piston unit of 12 h.p., each cylinder containing two pistons; a rare feature most familiar in the Gobron-Brillié. Murray's low-tension chain-driven magneto ignition was another unconventional point in a car that was full of idiosyncrasies. Its high wheels, solid tyres, and dogcart body combined to produce an uncompromisingly horseless-carriage aspect at a time when this was out of date, but the Arrol-Johnston's lack of respect for fashion was outweighed by its strength and straightforwardness of construction, which led to reliability and long life. Though the type was both expensive and inefficient, 3 litres of slow-turning engine generating only enough power from 800 r.p.m. to propel over a ton of car at 20 m.p.h., it was made until 1905, by which time it was truly archaic. In the same year, indeed, a new model with a front engine and shaft drive to a live rear axle had appeared alongside it.

51 FRATELLI CEIRANO,
1901, Italy

Giovanni Ceirano in 1899 made a car for the Welleyes bicycle concern of

Turin, which was used as the basis for the first F.I.A.T. car when that firm took over Welleyes over. He went to work for F.I.A.T., but in later life Giovanni was responsible for the S.C.A.T., Junior and Rapid cars, while a brother Matteo made the Itala and the S.P.A. The prolific Ceirano family between them also produced three makes of cars bearing the family name, one of which is illustrated. This was a joint effort by Matteo and another brother, Giovanni Battista. The Fratelli Ceirano was typical of Italian small-car practice of the time in being a copy of French design, in this case Renault and Darracq (54, 55), powered by an imported French Aster engine. The latter produced 5 b.h.p. at 800 r.p.m. The little car, of which the example illustrated is in the Museo dell'Automobile, Turin, weighed little more than 7 cwt.

52 LUC COURT, 1901,
France

Luc Court et Cie were set up in 1892 to make electrical equipment, and in 1901 began to build cars and engines. The 8-h.p. model shown, like others of the make, was remarkable for two features —its five-speed gear-box, and the 'double-chassis' system of Louis-Paul Lecoin, which allowed rapid changes of body style. The car illustrated weighed rather over 14 cwt., and was capable of 34 m.p.h.

53 CORRE, 1901, France

The Société des Automobiles Corre started life around 1899 by selling

Peugeot, De Dion-Bouton, and Renault cars (8, 32, 54), and making their own motor-tricycles and quadricycles. Monsieur J. Corre built his first cars in 1901, mainly from assembled Renault parts, including De Dion or Aster engines. Mutel engines were also used. As an assembler, Corre would have bought wherever he liked to buy, and could buy. By 1902 some of his cars used the 864-c.c. 8-h.p. De Dion engine. He went in for *voiturette* (light car) racing enthusiastically, putting up unspectacular, if regular performances. His racing cars of 1902 were fitted with either the 8-h.p. De Dion unit, or the 9-h.p. Aster. In the following year 12-h.p., $2\frac{1}{2}$-litre twins were seen, and also a four-cylinder, 16-h.p. machine in the *voiture légère* class (the next heaviest). By 1905 Corre's touring cars were also powered by bigger engines, including (as well as the faithful old 8-h.p. De Dion) 12- and 24-h.p. units by the same manufacturer. His later racers came in all sizes, from De Dion-based *voiturettes* for the Coupe de *L'Auto* races to monster *grandes voitures* such as the 70 h.p. for the 1906 Circuit des Ardennes and the 80 h.p. for the 1907 Grand Prix. By the latter year the firm was under different management, and was making a line of fast small cars called Corre-La Licornes.

54 RENAULT, 1901, France

Louis, Marcel, and Fernand Renault were the sons of a wealthy linen draper. Marcel and Fernand pursued their father's métier, but Louis, a motor-tricycle enthusiast who had bought a De Dion (32) in 1897, built an experimental four-wheeled light car in 1898. The Renault's transmission set the pattern for small cars of its period; a pattern which spread to all types of car. In the front of a tubular chassis, he installed a $1\frac{3}{4}$-h.p. De Dion-Bouton engine which drove to the rear wheels via a friction clutch, a gear-box, and a shaft. Thence the drive was taken by jointed shaft to a spring live axle. The tumbler-action gear-box gave direct drive on top. Louis Renault was the first to provide this combination of features, that subsequently became the norm. With his brothers as partners, Louis put his tiny car into production at Billancourt in 1899. By mid-1899, sixty examples had been delivered. A $2\frac{1}{4}$-h.p. engine was available in the same year, followed in 1900 by ones of $3\frac{1}{2}$ and 5 h.p., the former still by De Dion. Aster engines were also supplied. Proprietary units were offered until 1904, but in the previous year, Renault began to make his own engines as well. By 1900 air-cooling had gone, and engines were water-cooled, with gilled-tube radiator elements on either side of the hood; also, a steering wheel was provided. This is the type illustrated. The car was far from cheap, but weighing only 4 cwt., it was a good performer in its class, being capable of around 24 m.p.h. In Italy, it was first imported and then assembled by the new firm of Isotta-Fraschini.

55 DARRACQ, 1901, France

Alexandre Darracq was the manufacturer of the highly successful Gladiator bicycle, with which he competed against British cycle imports into France in the 1890s. He sold his business in 1896, going first into cycle component manufacture, and then turning his attention to motor-cars. He had already carried out an abortive foray into the field of motor vehicles in 1894, with the Millet motor-cycle. His aim was to make a good car in numbers sufficient to bring the price within the reach of a wider market than had hitherto been touched by the young industry. He first commissioned Léon Bollée to design him a car, but this four-wheeler of 1898, though a great improvement on Bollée's famous but much less sophisticated three-wheeled *voiturette* (29), was still belt-driven, so was obsolescent to begin with. Success came to Darracq when he adopted the Renault layout (54), using a $6\frac{1}{2}$-h.p. vertical engine at the front, a three-speed gear-box, and shaft drive to a live rear axle. The gear-box was of normal sliding-pinion type, unlike that in the Renault, and the inlet valve had variable lift for greater engine flexibility. Production began in 1900. The Suresnes factory turned out no fewer than 1200 examples in 1901 alone, for although the Darracq was noisy, it was lively and really cheap. In the following year a bigger single-cylinder model replaced it, and was accompanied by a 9-h.p. twin.

56 MORS, 1901, France

Emile Mors, an electrical engineer at the head of a business that had been founded in 1851, made some gasoline railcars in 1892–3, and built his first motor-car three years later. It was a Benz-like machine (40), though with belt final drive. In 1897, however, he produced a wholly original and very sophisticated design, powered by a rear-mounted vee-four engine (the first in a production car) sparked by low-tension ignition from a dynamo and battery. This was the world's earliest successful car dynamo. It charged the battery or worked the ignition. A front-engined flat-twin *voiturette* followed, current in 1899 and 1900. From 1899 normal low-tension magneto ignition was available. The Panhard type of car illustrated was designed by Henri Brasier, and was seen at first in 1899 with the old engines. By 1901 it had acquired a four-cylinder in-line 10-h.p. unit and became the most successful Mors to date, being completely conventional yet (like all of its breed) very well made. Most of the make's fame came from its string of major racing successes, in which it was the Panhard-Levassor's nearest rival. Its most outstanding wins were in the 1901 Paris–Berlin Race, and the 1903 Paris–Madrid event, which was stopped at Bordeaux after several fatal accidents. The Mors in this race were the first cars to wear shock-absorbers.

57 CLÉMENT GLADIATOR, 1901, France

Alexandre Darracq's Gladiator bicycle factory was sold in 1896 to interests which amalgamated with Adolphe Clément to form the Clément-Gladiator Company. The first car it produced was the $3\frac{1}{4}$-h.p. model of 1900, which was fitted with a single-cylinder Aster engine, two-speed epicyclic gearing, and both primary and final drive by

chain. This unusual little beast was followed by the rather more ortho-dox type illustrated, with its De Dion-Bouton engine (32) of $2\frac{1}{4}$ h.p. This car, which is in the Museon di Rodo at Uzès, weighed less than 3 cwt., and was capable of 20 m.p.h. From 1901 there was also a $6\frac{1}{2}$-h.p. Aster-engined vehicle. At the end of 1901 the engineer Marius Barbarou joined the firm to design a more modern range (82).

58 DELAHAYE, 1901, France

Emile Delahaye built his first car in 1893-4, showing it to the public in 1895, and putting it on sale in the following year. It had a great deal in common with the Benz (40), a resemblance that persisted well after the German car had gone out of fashion. The type shown, which offered variety in bodywork and other detail, was made from 1900 to 1902, by which time, with its big, slow-running single-cylinder horizontal engine of $4\frac{1}{2}$ h.p. at the rear, its 20 m.p.h. maximum, and its belt drive, it was something of a dinosaur. Contrast this car with the very modern Renault (54), of the same generation. This did not stop Delahaye et Cie from asking a high price for it. They listed a 9-h.p. two-cylinder version, with three or four forward speeds, from 1898, but Benz had anticipated them. The last horizontal-engined Delahayes were turned out in 1902, but the firm continued to make cars of conventional, not to say conservative design until 1935, when the famous Type 135 sports car so unexpectedly arrived.

59 SCANIA, 1901, Sweden

The Maskin A.B. Scania of Malmo made British Humber bicycles under licence from 1900, but as early as 1894, they had imported and studied a Hildebrand & Wolfmuller motor-cycle from Germany. A motor-car, designed by Fridolf Thorssin on orthodox lines, followed in 1901. This type, the one illustrated, is still existent in the Tekniska Museet, Stockholm. The engine used was made by Kämper of Germany. The latter was also the case with the next model, of which a series of six was laid down in 1902; this was a front-engined car designed by Anton Svenson. In 1902 as well, however, the company built the first engine of their own design. It was an air-cooled vertical twin with mechanically-operated inlet valves, developing 6 h.p.

60 MERCEDES, 1901, Germany

The Daimler Motoren Gesellschaft's new model of 1901, which was to become famous as the progenitor of the shape of the modern motor-car and of some of its basic handling and running qualities, did not spring up fully formed like Venus from the waves. Daimler took their first steps towards an up-to-date (not novel) design in 1897 when they adopted the Panhard-Levassor (13) system—a vertical two-cylinder 'Phoenix' engine at the front, a cone clutch, a sliding-pinion gear-box, chain final drive, a gilled-tube radiator, and Ackermann steering. In 1898 these Daimlers improved on the Panhard by adopting Simms-Bosch low-tension

ignition, and later cars had a form of honeycomb radiator. The latter feature, too, was found on the small Daimler designed by Gottlieb's son Paul in 1899, and put into production in the next year as the PD-Wagen. In 1899, prompted by Emil Jellinek, the Austrian Consul in Nice, Daimler agent and far-sighted, wealthy sportsman, the company built their first racing car. This 24-h.p. machine had the honeycomb radiator, underslung at the front, and two new features in the shape of a pressed-steel frame (instead of the normal metal-reinforced wood or steel tube) and a gate-type gear-change. Although Jellinek and his customers raced the car, which was put into production, it was far too fast for its conventionally short wheelbase and high centre of gravity. Jellinek asked for something better, and in 1901, by which time the dead Gottlieb Daimler's conservative influence had been superseded by that of the progressive Wilhelm Maybach, he got it. Proper control of a specialized high-performance car was the immediate object—control of the most powerful engine so far seen in a production car, and control of the car as a whole. That it started a revolution was a by-product of the fact that the achievement of this aim produced the best all-purpose car the world had seen. The 24-h.p. engine was refined and enlarged, reappearing in the new car as the 35 h.p. with mechanically-operated inlet valves with variable lift, that with the low-tension magneto ignition and efficient carburation already supplied, gave it unparalleled flexibility and smoothness. Mechanically-operated inlet valves were not new in themselves, having been used in the Markus car of 1875–7 (2), in the first Benz of 1886 (6), and in the 1896 Lanchester (23), but they were certainly novel in this latest form, and in its effect. Induction throttling was soon substituted for variable valve lift, with the same result. For safer handling at speed, the car was made much longer and lower than the old 24 h.p., and also the honeycomb radiator was raised to the front of the engine, so giving the new car a profile that was different from that of all others. Earlier features retained were the pressed-steel frame and gate-type gear-change. The indicated power was produced at 1000 r.p.m. which was not a specially high speed for 1901, but sufficed to give the car a top speed of around 50 m.p.h. Not surprisingly, this superlative machine was extremely expensive. However, being easy and pleasant to drive as well as fast, it was suitable for all kinds of motoring, not merely racing. Jellinek had raced the 24-h.p. car under the gentleman-driver's *nom de guerre* of Mercedes, his daughter's name, and he named the new car after her. Originally it was to be called the Mercedes only in certain countries of Europe and in the U.S.A., but the name came to be applied to it everywhere, and then to all models from Canstatt. Jellinek had contracted with Daimler to buy the whole first year's output for resale, and after teething troubles had been ironed out, his confidence was fully justified by its overwhelming success among the wealthy. Many of Jellinek's customers for the first Mercedes model were Americans, for whom the cars were imported and assembled by William Steinway in New York. The Mercedes started the fashion for foreign cars

among well-to-do Americans, to whom it was smart to own one. Within a couple of years manufacturers in both Europe and America of the more expensive type of car were having to follow the Mercedes pattern in order to avoid being out of date. The revolution was under way in this field, just as Renault (54) had started one among cheap cars.

61 MAURER UNION, 1901, Germany

Ludwig Maurer's little friction-drive *voiturette* was offered by the Automobilwerke Union A.G. of Nuremburg. The single-cylinder model, which was made until 1908 with minor modifications, developed 6 h.p. at 800 r.p.m., weighed just under 5 cwt., and was capable of rather over 25 m.p.h. Some Maurer Unions had double friction disc transmission. Cars made until 1903 had De Dion-Bouton engines (32). A two-cylinder model arrived in 1902, and a four in 1905.

62 DURKOPP, 1901, Germany

Nikolaus Durkopp of Bielefeld started to make cars in 1898, with a light *voiturette*, as the smallest type of car was then generally known, and two bigger machines. The latter were made under Panhard-Levassor licence (73) until 1901, and were known as Canello-Durkopps, from Canellopoulos, their designer, a French engineer. They were sold as the Watsonia in Britain by Dr Lehwess, who was the first man to try to drive a car (not a Durkopp) round the world. The model illustrated, the 8-h.p. twin, weighed a little over 13 cwt., and was introduced in 1901 together with a four-cylinder machine, and represented a breakaway from purely French origins. Durkopps made a name for high quality, and also built public service vehicles.

63 **COLUMBIA**, 1901, U.S.A.

Henry G. Morris and Pedro G. Salom built electric carriages in Philadelphia, which they called Electrobats. They founded the Electric Carriage & Wagon Company, which in 1897 was supplying New York with taxi-cabs. They sold out to the Electric Storage Battery Company, which was reorganized as the Electric Vehicle Company. Expansion came with a merger in 1899 with the Pope Manufacturing Company, America's biggest bicycle manufacturers, who had also been experimenting with motor vehicles. While the Electric Vehicle Company went on to make no fewer than 2000 cabs, under the name of Columbia (and also electric passenger cars), the Pope Manufacturing Company also supported the efforts of Hiram Percy Maxim to produce gasoline-engined vehicles. These cars were also called Columbias. That illustrated was, for America at this time, an unusually sophisticated design, with its high-speed vertical engine and three-speed sliding-pinion gear-box. Claimed output was 5 b.h.p., and the maximum speed was a true 35 m.p.h., which suggests a higher output, and a higher efficiency than the engines in the Oldsmobile (74), Rambler (75), Winton (76) and Packard (77). Wheel steering, too,

was unusual in America at this date, though the feature of automatic ignition advance was shared with the Packard. Hiram Percy Maxim was the son of Sir Hiram Maxim, who built a steam aeroplane and invented the Maxim machine-gun.

64 **KNOX**, 1901, U.S.A.

The car illustrated was the best-known product of the Knox Automobile Company of Springfield, Massachusetts. It was a three-wheeler, a rare bird indeed in America, and its 4-h.p. engine was air-cooled with the help of a bristle of copper pins screwed into the cylinder-barrel, in place of the usual fins. The model was made until 1903. A four-wheeler first appeared in 1901, and later Knoxes (which were made up to 1915) could be had with water-cooling. None had the character of the curious little tricycle that first made the company's name, and that of the 'Knox Waterless', as its air-cooled cars were called.

65 **PANHARD-LEVASSOR,**
6–7 h.p., 1902, France

The Panhard-Levassor design had developed in several directions since the 1895 type was introduced (13). In 1898 handling and control at speed was much improved by the introduction of pneumatic tyres, of castor effect in the steering, which for the first time gave Panhard steering a self-centring action, and of a raked steering wheel. A gilled-tube radiator was fitted at the rear, and moved to the front of the car a year later. A four-cylinder version of the Phoenix engine, with bore and stroke of 90 by 130 mm., had been introduced in 1896, then dropped until 1898, when a two-cylinder of the same dimensions was also available. The latter unit, developing 6–7 b.h.p. at 700–800 r.p.m., was fitted to a new model introduced in 1901 for 1902 and illustrated here. This car featured the option of electric or hot-tube ignition. The former was becoming more popular, as it allowed the engine far greater flexibility of running. The maximum speed in three-speed form was upwards of 30 m.p.h., and 40 m.p.h. with four speeds.

66 GEORGES RICHARD,
1902, France

Georges Richard et Cie of Paris made their first car in 1898. By the following year, two models, a 7 h.p. and a 10 h.p., were being offered to the public, both basically similar, both being built under Benz (40) licence. A front-mounted two-cylinder engine driven by belts and chains, and the option of three or four forward speeds was listed. In 1900 Georges Richard abandoned the Benz design in favour of that of the Belgian Vivinus (42), making a car with a $3\frac{1}{2}$-h.p. vertical single-cylinder engine, air-cooled, with belt drive. In 1901 followed another non-original design, that illustrated, in which Georges Richard, like so many other manufacturers, looked to the Panhard-Levassor (13) for inspiration; although in this particular car, a De Dion engine has been substituted. An engine at the front drove through a cone clutch, sliding-pinion gear-box and side

chains. In 1903 the model acquired four forward speeds, and low-tension magneto ignition. The Vivinus-type machine was still made as late as 1902, though the year before the engineer Henri Brasier, formerly of Mors (56), joined the company, and the vehicles were renamed Richard-Brasiers. It was he who was responsible for the racing cars that won the 1904 and 1905 Gordon Bennett races in the hands of Théry. Surprisingly, even the Benz-type cars had been very successful in racing before the turn of the century. Georges Richard departed by 1905 to make the Unic, and the automobiles he left behind were henceforth called Brasiers.

67 PEUGEOT, 1902, France

Les Fils de Peugeot Frères were a long time in adopting a modern design in their cars, but they got around to it at last at the time of the 1901 Paris Salon, by which stage the faithful old type with rear horizontal engine and tube ignition (9) had been dropped. Some Peugeot racing cars had been of more modern design already, but the 1902 range now shown were the first front vertical-engined production machines. The most popular was the 5 h.p. illustrated, though an 8-h.p. twin and a 15-h.p. four with mechanically-operated inlet valves was also offered. This 'Bébé' Peugeot at first had only two forward speeds, but in late 1902 the number was increased to three, in the so-called 6 h.p., which in fact was otherwise little altered. The engine actually developed some $6\frac{1}{2}$ b.h.p. at 1000 r.p.m., providing the half-ton car with a very respectable maximum speed of about 30 m.p.h. It was current until 1904. The machine sold well in Britain. It was handled there by Charles Friswell.

68 **GILLET-FOREST**, 1902, France

The Société Gillet-Forest of Saint-Cloud dated from 1889, and started car manufacture in 1900 with a shaft-driven 5-h.p. *voiturette*. The type illustrated that followed it developed 7 h.p. at 700 r.p.m., or $8\frac{1}{2}$ h.p. at the maximum engine speed of 100 r.p.m., from a motor of the company's own construction. The Gillet-Forest's most distinctive exterior feature was its curved tubular radiator, which also acted as a condenser of steam collected from the cylinder water-jacket and used for cooling. The horizontal engine and idiosyncratic cooling arrangements were dropped from 1905, except on the company's commercial vehicles.

69 **DE DIETRICH**, 1902, France

The firm of De Dietrich et Cie was established in 1769. At the time of the Franco-Prussian War of 1870-1 they were iron and steel manufacturers, forced by the war to move their headquarters from Alsace to Lunéville in Lorraine. They later became famous as builders of railroad locomotives, who under Baron Adrien de Turckheim started to make cars as well. At first, the Baron turned to Amédée Bollée, jun., who designed him a light machine with

belt (later belt-and-chain) drive. This was an obsolescent design, and the Lunéville works next engaged Turcat and Méry of Marseilles as consulting engineers. These gentlemen were already building their own Turcat-Méry car, on Panhard-Levassor lines (13), and continued to do so while they produced very similar cars for De Dietrich. This was in 1902. At this time, four Turcat-Méry types of De Dietrich were made; an 8-h.p. twin, and fours of 12, 16, and 24 h.p. A 16-h.p. car is illustrated. It was a conservative design by this time, with its armoured wood frame and gilled-tube radiator, but was a fair performer for its day, its engine turning at up to 1200 r.p.m., producing around 18 b.h.p. and propelling the car at up to 45 m.p.h. The model was made until 1904, when the whole range was modernized with steel frames and mechanically-operated inlet valves *à la* Mercedes (60). Meanwhile at the company's other works at Niederbronn in German Alsace, then part of Germany, the Vivinus from Belgium (42) had been built under licence from 1900 as a De Dietrich, and from 1903 there emanated from it 24-h.p. and 30-h.p. designs by the young Ettore Bugatti. Like the Lunéville cars, Bugatti's were well made, fast, reliable, and expensive, if not quite as conventional. In 1905, however, the Niederbronn works were closed, production was concentrated at Lunéville, and the cars were eventually renamed Lorraine-Dietrichs.

70 **ADER**, 1902, France

Clement Ader, the pioneer aviator, claimed to have been the first man to fly in a powered heavier-than-air aircraft; a steam-propelled machine. However, cars were also made to his designs, by the Société Industrielle des Telephones-Voitures Automobiles Système Ader of Levallois from 1901. Early Aders were distinguished by the vee formation of their cylinders, which were either vee-twins or vee-fours. They were made until about 1906, and were sold as the Pegasus in Britain. Some racing Aders were further notable for their independent front suspension by a transverse spring, after the manner of the Decauville (26). A competitor in the *voiturette* (smallest) class of the 1903 Paris–Madrid Race had the engine dimensions of the car illustrated (the 8 h.p.-model, made in 1902 and 1903), but double the number of cylinders, still in vee, while another Ader in the same race, but running in the *voiture légère* class (the next size up) had eight vee cylinders of the same size totalling 3618 c.c.

71 **BERNA**, 1902,
Switzerland

Joseph Wyss, an ornamental ironworker of Berne, built his first car in 1902. It was virtually identical to the De Dion-Bouton from France (32), incorporating that car's type of engine, gear-change, and transmission system. This machine, now to be seen in the Verkehrshaus der Schweiz in Lucerne, was fitted with a body by Geissberger of Zurich. The $5\frac{1}{4}$-h.p. engine propelled the 5-cwt. car at around 25 m.p.h. In 1903 there followed an 8 h.p. with a front engine, which sounds very much like the 8 h.p. De Dion then current.

Later, commercial vehicles only were made, and are still offered.

72 **WEBER**, 1902,
Switzerland

J. Weber et Cie of Uster were textile machinery manufacturers who in 1899 took up motor manufacture. As was common among firms new to mechanical transportation, they chose to follow an existing pattern, making the three-wheeled Rapid from Zurich under licence; a vehicle that was itself based on the Léon Bollée (31) from France. It had a water-cooled 3-h.p. engine with belt drive and the crude Bollée clutch action by means of moving the rear wheel, and was made in considerable numbers. A four-wheeler of more conventional pattern, with 6/8-h.p. vertical single-cylinder engine and shaft drive followed, but then the engine, now of 12 h.p., migrated to the rear and stayed there until production ceased in 1906. The car illustrated is one of this type. It is a little surprising to find that these vehicles, which were very expensive, were built at the rate of sixty a year.

73 **WOLSELEY**, 1902,
Great Britain

While employed by the Wolseley Sheep Shearing Machine Company of Birmingham, Herbert Austin made their first car. It was an air-cooled three-wheeler based on the Léon Bollée from France (31). An improved machine with a water-cooled, two-cylinder engine and a single front wheel appeared in the same year of 1896, and three years later Austin built a four-wheeler, with front water-cooled engine of $3\frac{1}{2}$ h.p., belt primary drive to a sliding-pinion gear-box, chain final drive, and tiller steering. This was the prototype for the first production Wolseley of 1900, which was the $4\frac{1}{2}$ h.p., renamed the 5 h.p. in 1901. This car had only one cylinder, but its transmission arrangements (by chain throughout) were the same as those in the car illustrated, the 10-h.p. model, except that it had three forward speeds instead of four. It had wheel steering. The 10 h.p. was first seen in 1900 as the 8 h.p., but in fact its engine developed 10 b.h.p. at a conservative 750 r.p.m. A solid machine, it weighed 19 cwt., but was capable of 24 m.p.h. and was listed from 1901 to 1906 (as the 12 h.p. from 1904). It was the most popular of the flat-twin Wolseleys, contributing more than any other model to the company's position as Britain's biggest motor manufacturer in 1902. Since 1901 this had been the Wolseley Tool & Motor Car Company, set up specifically to build cars. Until 1906 there were plentiful variants on the horizontal-engined theme, with one, two, and four cylinders. Strongly-built, reliable and simple, with low-stressed, slow-turning, sizeable engines, these cars had something in common with the contemporary American 'gas-buggies', and were popular for much the same reasons, but they, too, fell from grace eventually because they were too slow, rough-running, and old-fashioned. They were replaced by conventional vertical-engined cars. Herbert Austin departed as a result of this change of policy, but his own first cars, when they appeared, showed that he had seen the light as well.

74 OLDSMOBILE, 1902, U.S.A.

Ransom Eli Olds began experimenting with a gasoline-engined car in 1896, having earlier made a steam car. The earliest Oldsmobile to go into production was also the most famous—the so-called 'Curved Dash' Olds, which was on sale from 1901. Its specification was in fundamentals typical of the simple 'gas-buggies' that were the typical American cars of the time. Its slow-running single-cylinder engine was capable of a maximum rotation of 500 r.p.m., developing around 5 b.h.p. at that speed. This sufficed to propel the little 7-cwt. car at 20 m.p.h. The gears were made by the Dodge brothers, who made components before they made complete cars. The suspension was curious: two long half-elliptic springs ran the full length of the very short wheelbase. At the front was a transverse spring. It acted as a shock-absorber for the tiller steering, which though direct, allowed excellent control and manoeuvrability. This Oldsmobile could be said to have 'arrived' when it provoked the world's first popular song devoted to one car; thenceforth, it was the 'Merry Oldsmobile'. Olds was a pioneer in a far more important sense; he was one of the first men to apply some quantity production techniques to the automobile. Six hundred cars were turned out in 1901, 2500 in 1902, 4000 in 1903, and 5000 in 1904. Dummy hoods and wheel steering could be had in the last year in response to the demands of fashion, while engine size had crept up to 7 h.p. and then to 9 h.p. Olds left his firm to make the very similar Reo, after a disagreement with his backers, but the Oldsmobile continued to be made in its old form until 1907, alongside newer, more conventional two-cylinder and four-cylinder models.

75 RAMBLER, 1902, U.S.A.

Thomas B. Jeffery was an Englishman who made bicycles in Chicago between 1878 and 1900. He built his first car in 1897, and other prototypes followed until 1902, when he sold his bicycle business and offered his first production car, which is illustrated. Construction at the Kenosha, Wisconsin works was in the hands of Charles T. Jeffery, Thomas' son. The engine of this otherwise typical 'gas-buggy' of the age was unusual in having a detachable cylinder-head and a mechanically-operated inlet valve. The hood was a dummy, there in deference to fashion, but doing duty as a tool-box. This Model C Rambler was heavy at $13\frac{1}{4}$ cwt., but its 6 b.h.p., produced at 1200 r.p.m., gave it a maximum speed of 30 m.p.h. The Model C sold no fewer than 1500 units in 1902. Rambler was, in fact, second in the American quantity–production field after Oldsmobile (74). 1903 saw a drop in sales to 1300, but they soared in 1904 to 2342 cars. In that year, wheel steering was adopted, a feature not seen since the Rambler prototypes had it, but already owners had taken advantage of the conversion kits available. Alongside the single-cylinder car, a bigger 15-h.p. model, the Model E, had made its bow in 1903.

76 WINTON, 1902, U.S.A.

Alexander Winton was a Scots bicycle maker who went into business in 1890 in Cleveland, Ohio. His first car, a prototype, was made in 1897, and was followed immediately by half a dozen motor-buses. These were dropped and the car put into production in 1898 by the Winton Motor Carriage Company, which sold twenty-two cars in its first eight months and two years later was one of the biggest motor manufacturers in the U.S.A. At one stage, ten cars a day were being turned out. The Winton owed its popularity to the qualities of simplicity and reliability that it shared with other 'gas-buggies' and to the sheer size of its engine, which gave it more power than most. A 15-h.p. twin was followed in 1902 by the 20 h.p. illustrated. With an engine speed of 1400 r.p.m., sufficient power was generated to propel the 20 h.p. at 37 m.p.h., which was a good deal faster than its American contemporaries. The company's first vertical-engined car appeared in 1901, but the horizontal-engined machine was made as late as 1905. Part of the early success of the make was due to spectacular publicity, which included the first motor drive across the U.S.A., by a 20 h.p. in 1903, and America's first participation in a motor race abroad, the Gordon Bennett event of 1900.

77 PACKARD, 1902, U.S.A.

James Ward Packard's Packard Electrical Company was founded in 1890 to make electric lamps. He was planning a car as early as 1893, however, and the first one, an experimental machine known as the Model A, was running by the end of 1899. It was inspired partly by the Winton (76), and partly by a De Dion-Bouton tricycle (32) that Packard had imported. This vehicle had a 12-h.p. engine, with automatic ignition advance, and tiller steering. The Model B that followed in 1900, also a prototype only, was similar. It weighed rather over 8 cwt., and was capable of 22 m.p.h. Encouraged by his success, James Ward Packard, with his brother Warren Dowd Packard, and George L. Weiss and W. A. Thatcher (both formerly of Winton), in 1900 formed the New York & Ohio Automobile Company at Warren, Ohio, to make cars. The first production type, Model C, is illustrated. It had wheel steering, and a slightly larger engine, but was otherwise virtually unchanged. The Packard was a typical 'gas-buggy' like most other American cars of the time, but was more refined than most in having three forward speeds. The single-cylinder Packard was made until 1904, the last type, the Model F, having a transverse front spring, but in that year, the first conventional four-cylinder car was offered, and the association of the name with big, expensive machines of fine quality had begun. This move came shortly after the Packard Motor Company was formed at Detroit.

78 BAKER, 1902, U.S.A.

Walter C. Baker, who worked for a ball-bearing manufacturer, built his first electric car in 1898. This buggy-like little vehicle used a 10-cell battery and a $\frac{3}{4}$-h.p. motor, and there were two for-ward speeds. The range was fifty miles' and maximum speed 20 m.p.h. In 1899 the Baker Motor Vehicle Company was founded at Cleveland, Ohio, and the car illustrated, with a slightly more powerful motor and three forward speeds, was put into production, remaining current until 1905. Ball-bearings were employed throughout, as might be supposed. The company also made commercial vehicles, but it was best known for the sensational Baker Electric Torpedo of 1902, a streamlined record-breaking machine that cost $10,000 to build and was timed at 104 m.p.h. when attacking the kilometre record. In 1915 the firm amalgamated with another electric vehicle manufacturer, Rauch & Lang, to form Baker, Rauch & Lang. This firm absorbed the makers of the Owen Magnetic car, with its Entz electric transmission and gasoline engine, and made it from 1915 to 1919.

79 F.I.A.T., 1902, Italy

The 12-h.p. model illustrated was F.I.A.T.'s second basic model, superseding the rear-engined car (35) designed by Aristide Faccioli. The latter had been fitted with successively bigger engines of 6 and 8 h.p., which were more successful than the first $3\frac{1}{2}$-h.p. car, proving the popularity of more power. At the Paris Salon of 1900 the company showed a new, more modern design with a front-mounted, four-cylinder engine and a honeycomb radiator as a prototype. Experiments were made in other directions, too, a front-engined 8-h.p. car with gilled-tube radiator taking part in the Giro d'Italia of 1901. Giovanni Enrico replaced

Faccioli as designer in 1901, and his first car, the 12 h.p., confirmed the change in company policy when it appeared late that year. A few early examples only had gilled-tube radiators. Four models were available in 1902; the old rear-engined 8 h.p., and fours in 12-, 16-, and 24-h.p. form. With the last three types, F.I.A.T. went from strength to strength. Only seventy-three cars had been made in 1901, but 134 in 1903. The company's first export, to France, was made in the former year; in 1902 twenty-five four-cylinder chassis were exported to Britain; and in 1903 the U.S.A. took her first F.I.A.T.s. The big, faster, more modern type had achieved this. The 12 h.p. in fact developed around 14 b.h.p. at 1200 r.p.m., and weighed something under 24 cwt. It acquired mechanically-operated inlet valves at the end of 1902. The 16 h.p., with over 4 litres, four forward speeds, and a plate clutch, was good for about 45 m.p.h., while the 24 h.p. had a 7·4-litre engine.

80 MARCHAND, 1902, Italy

The firm of Orio e Marchand of Piacenza was founded in 1899. They started by making motor-cycles, but at the end of 1898 turned to cars, building the Decauville from France (26) under licence. Stefano Orio died in 1899, and the brothers Marchand took over. The 1899 Marchand was a 5-h.p. machine with two cylinders in vee formation. This was followed by the vertical-twin 10 h.p. of 1902–3, which is illustrated. In turn, it was superseded by a type with a vertical four-cylinder engine and four forward speeds. Later on, the

company was associated with Dufaux of Switzerland, making a car called the Dufaux-Marchand for a couple of years.

81 WARTBURG, 1902, Germany

Heinrich Ehrhardt, an armaments manufacturer, launched the Fahrzeug-fabrik Eisenach in 1896. It produced its first cars, which were powered by electricity, in 1898. They were called Eisenachs, after the town where they were made. From the same year the Decauville from France (26) was built under licence. These cars were named Wartburgwagen after the castle above Eisenach. By 1900 150 examples had been made, and a front-engined version had been introduced. From 1901 there were two-cylinder Wartburgs of $5\frac{1}{2}$, $6\frac{1}{2}$, and $8\frac{1}{2}$ h.p., only the first-named with a rear engine, and also (in 1902) a four-cylinder car, all on Decauville lines. That illustrated is the $5\frac{1}{2}$-h.p. model, on sale until 1903. It developed its power at 100 r.p.m., weighed rather under 9 cwt., and could reach 20 m.p.h. It was typical of French-derived German small-car practice of the time, except in that it copied the Decauville's independent front suspension. In 1904 the Ehrhardt connection ended, the Decauville designs were dropped, and an original type introduced. This new line was known as the Dixi—'I have spoken' —the last word had been said.

82 GLADIATOR, 1903, France

Adolphe Clément's Clément-Gladiator Company offered the public *voiturettes* until 1902 (57). At the end of the previous year, however, the engineer Marius Barbarou joined the firm, bigger cars arrived also, and the company expanded. Around this time there were 1200 workmen in the Pré-St Gervais factory near Paris. Some of the new line were cars cast in a traditional mould, with automatic inlet valves, chain drive, trembler-coil ignition, and wood frames. Barbarou's time with Clément-Gladiator also saw the introduction of a modern range—a 9-h.p. twin and two fours of 12 and 16 h.p.—with mechanically-operated inlet valves, shaft drive, low-tension magneto ignition, and steel frames. By 1903 both Clément and Barbarou had departed, the one to make cars called Clément-Bayard or simply Clément, the other to design the Parsifal-type Benz for the Mannheim concern (92). Their former company's vehicles continued under the name of Gladiator, some being made under licence by Austin of England in 1909.

83 LANCHESTER, 1903,
Great Britain

The car illustrated was one of the first type to be put into production by the Lanchester brothers. It was based closely upon the three prototypes (23). The Lanchester Engine Company began to turn it out late in 1900, starting with a batch of six, and the car was available as late as 1908 to special order. It differed mainly from the prototypes in having a larger engine, rated at 10 h.p.; in the lower part of the body being integral with the frame members (instead of using a tubular frame and a

separate body); and in its three-speed transmission. In spite of its unconventional character, the Lanchester's very sophisticated and efficient specification quickly attracted a devoted if limited following. The car's silence and smoothness, especially for an air-cooled twin, was remarkable. It handled well, a factor helped by the very steady, self-centering steering; it was exceptionally comfortable, thanks to excellent cantilever springing at front and rear; and with all this luxury, it was fast, with a 35-m.p.h. maximum. A water-cooled engine became optional from 1902. It was rated at 12 h.p. because the air-cooling fans, greedy of power, were dropped; and in fact although the water-cooled car was larger, and weighed 21 cwt. instead of 17 cwt., it was faster, with a 40 m.p.h. maximum. In 1904 both types were available with a bigger engine, thanks to a larger bore of 146 mm.

84 STANDARD, 1903,
Great Britain

R. W. Maudslay was a civil engineer, who took to motor-car manufacture in Coventry in 1903. Alex Craig, who had been a consulting engineer, now came to work for Maudslay full-time. The latter asked him for a 'standard' car, by which he meant one based on tried, tested, standardized design, in so far as that existed as early as 1903. Maudslay followed normal practice in this; most motor manufacturers, who at this time were entering a new and largely unexplored field, tended to play safe. In the event, Craig's earliest creation, illustrated here, was not all that conventional. Its engine was notably over-square, it used a mechanically-operated inlet valve in an L-head when such things were still exceptional in small cars, it was very flexible, and it could rev. up to 2000 r.p.m. The latter features no doubt helped a very small engine to rate 6 h.p. and to pull quite a lot of motor-car. The chassis frame was extremely rigid, too. The second car built was a two-cylinder rated at 12/15 h.p. No proper manufacture was undertaken until 1905; production was concentrated on engines for others. Standard cars only began to reach the public in appreciable quantities when Charles Friswell, a fine salesman, became their sole distributor. By this time, they were indeed 'standard' cars, full of merit in most directions, but quite lacking originality.

85 HUMBERETTE, 1903,
     Great Britain

Thomas Humber was a very early (1868) manufacturer of British bicycles, who became famous for his two-wheeled machinery, which was of excellent quality. The company promoter H. J. Lawson absorbed the company in 1896 and introduced it to motor manufacture, but the cars produced under his aegis were few, long delayed and mostly bad. Four years later Humber Ltd. were formed as an independent concern, and started to take the making of small cars seriously, but they were best known at first for their very good motor-cycle of 1901. The first successful and popular motor-car to emerge from the Coventry works was the little 5-h.p. Humberette of 1903. It

was based on the proven formula of the French De Dion-Bouton (32), with its tubular frame, water-cooled vertical single-cylinder engine at the front, and shaft drive to a live axle. In 1904 an improved version with a $6\frac{1}{2}$-h.p. engine and three forward speeds was offered alongside the earlier car; but both were dropped in 1905. The Humberette was eventually made in two factories—the more utility versions came from Coventry, and the dearer, better-equipped ones from Beeston. The firm also sold a motor-tricycle called the Humber Olympia Tandem at around the same time.

86 DAIMLER, 1903,
     Great Britain

The Daimler Motor Syndicate was founded by Frederick R. Simms in 1891 to exploit Daimler gasoline engines in Britain (4). In 1895 H. J. Lawson's British Motor Syndicate bought the British rights in the patents, selling them in the following year to the Daimler Motor Company, founded by Lawson to make cars of Daimler type. Operating from the Motor Mills, Coventry, the company began building cars on Daimler-*cum*-Panhard-Levassor lines (13) in 1897. They were inferior to either of their parents, being heavier, lower-geared, and more cumbersome. They were, however, very strongly built. Until 1901, two basic models were sold: a two-cylinder machine rated at $4\frac{1}{2}$ h.p., or 6 h.p. with electric ignition, and one with a four-cylinder engine with the same dimensions (90 by 120 mm.) called first an 8 h.p. and then a 12 h.p. One $4\frac{1}{2}$-h.p.

device was a deservedly little-known belt-driven light car called the 'Critchley' or 'Kimberley' model. The two chain-driven machines were capable of around 20 and 30 m.p.h. respectively. About 1900 came dual ignition and wheel steering. Driven by the Hon. John Scott-Montagu, a 12 h.p. which took third place in the Tourist Class of the 1899 Paris–Ostend Race was the first British car ever to participate in a foreign competition. Sales, never very great, declined from 1900. However, an American, Percy Martin, replaced J. S. Critchley as works manager, and at the end of 1901 a new, powerful 22-h.p. car arrived. One is illustrated. It and a new 12-h.p. four-cylinder replaced the two old cars. Both were much refined vehicles. The 22 h.p. had four forward speeds and the 12 h.p. three. With variations to the cylinder dimensions and ratings, they became the company's staple offerings. Percy Martin became managing director when the company was reformed in 1903, and it went from strength to strength. During 1904 a new range of four cars (effectively three, since few were made of the 7-h.p. twin) with coil or magneto ignition and mechanically-operated inlet valves was introduced. The 28/36 h.p. at the top end was the first Daimler to wear the famous cast aluminium ribbed radiator.

87 CADILLAC, 1903, U.S.A.

Henry M. Leland's Leland & Faulconer Manufacturing Company had made engines for Ransom E. Olds (74) and for the Detroit Automobile Company. Henry Ford made a few cars for the latter firm in 1902 (88), but later that year it became the Cadillac Automobile Company. By the end of 1902 the first fifty of Leland's Cadillacs were ready, and early in 1903 he began to sell this Model A to the public. The $6\frac{1}{2}$-h.p. engine was a typically American big, slow-running unit, with a normal régime of 750 r.p.m., but the car was unusual in its very high quality, which dated from the fine castings Leland had been making since 1895, and in having wheel steering from the first. Maximum speed was 25 m.p.h. The Cadillac was practical and reliable, and sold well not only in the U.S.A. but also in Britain, where it was promoted by F. S. Bennett, a good salesman who had handled the Oldsmobile (74) as well. In all, around 1700 Model As were sold. In 1904 came a dummy hood and a more powerful engine of 10 h.p. A team of these cars was used by Bennett to demonstrate Leland's proud boast that the parts of his cars were fully interchangeable; a rare achievement in the days of hand finishing. The Dewar Trophy rewarded him in 1908. The big single was continued until the following year, although the first four-cylinder Cadillac saw the light three years earlier.

88 FORD, 1903, U.S.A.

Henry Ford's first, experimental car dated from 1896 (18). His earliest attempt at automobile manufacture, with the Detroit Automobile Company from 1899, failed after only a few passenger vehicles were made. He obtained finance and public attention for his new Ford Motor Company thanks to the publicity gained by three special sprint cars, and the first Ford proper was offered to customers in 1903. This Model A, like most of its creator's later products, was aimed at the cheap-car market currently dominated by the Oldsmobile (74). It differed in no way from its main competitors, being a light buggy-type machine with a big, slow-turning engine. This, the chassis and the transmission were made by the Dodge brothers, who took an interest in the Ford Motor Company instead of payment. (Incidentally, they sold their $10,000 share to Ford in 1919 for $25 million.) Maximum speed was 30 m.p.h. In 1903, 1708 cars were made; an impressive total. The Models C and F that followed in 1904 had hoods and were improved types.

89 DURYEA, 1903, U.S.A.

Charles E. and Frank Duryea's Duryea Motor Wagon Company, the makers of what on present evidence is generally accepted as America's first working gasoline-engined road vehicle (8), died in 1898. The brothers had already parted. The firm's successor was the Duryea Power Company of Waterloo, Iowa, run by Charles E. Duryea. Its staple model for several years was a most original machine, of the type illustrated. The first car of 1898 had three wheels, but the rest had four. The 10-h.p. engine, in its later form with exactly square dimensions achieved by enlarging the bore and reducing the stroke, had three inclined cylinders with a *désaxé* crankshaft; the earliest known appearance of the latter feature. The power quoted was produced at a

modest 600 r.p.m. The car boasted 'one-hand' control: a lever tilted to steer, twisted to operate the throttle, and pushed down to change gear. The bodies were in highly unusual, opulently curvilinear shapes which tried to conceal the ingenious works beneath. The name was 'The Duryea Power Carriage'—this was a carriage, not a machine. It was 'The Ladies' Car'— 'The Doctors' Car'. The virtues stressed were elegance, comfort, silence, and simplicity. Unfortunately, the Duryea suffered from primitive lubrication, poor cooling, and poor finish. It was also too unconventional. The British-built Duryea was a better car, but even that did not last beyond 1907. Henry Sturmey had begun importing the American product in 1901, and three years later his British Duryea Company started manufacture, including some models peculiar to the British market, with British 12-, and 15-h.p. engines, both with mechanically-operated inlet valves. Sturmey also made a few four-cylinder, 18-h.p. machines. For its part, the parent company made a horizontally-opposed twin, as well as the three-cylinder, but the latter was always the main product.

90 FRANKLIN, 1903, U.S.A.

The H. H. Franklin Manufacturing Company sold its first car in 1902. This two-passenger Model A machine was in no way remarkable among its compatriots of the time, with its light construction and its two-speed epicyclic gearing and single-chain drive, except as regards its engine. This power unit was an in-line air-cooled four with separate finned cylinders, fixed heads, and mechanically-operated overhead exhaust valves, the pushrods of which passed through the exhaust down pipes from the cylinders. This engine produced about 7 b.h.p., and had a wide range of flexibility; from 300 to 1000 r.p.m. Thirteen cars were made in 1902; there was little change for 1903. With this model, the company was set from its very beginning on the course it was always to follow, favouring the multi-cylinder air-cooled engine until the end in 1934.

91 SCANIA, 1903, Sweden

Both the illustrations show 1903 types of the Maskin A.B. Scania of Malmo. They were basically similar, completely conventional machines. The upper illustration shows the more conservative model, with battery and trembler coil ignition, two forward speeds only, and an underslung gilled-tube radiator. The lower picture is of the three-speed type, with low-tension magneto ignition and a radiator in the 'modern' position. In addition to these 8 h.p. cars, it is said that a single-cylinder water-cooled 6 h.p. machine was also made. From the variety of types mentioned here and under (59) below, it can be seen that the company was feeling its way, making cars of different designs in penny packets.

92, 93 BENZ, 1903, Germany

The year 1902 saw the end of the faithful old line of belt-driven cars from

Mannheim (40). They were long obsolete—they had been rendered out of date three years before by De Dion-Bouton (32) and Renault (54)—and sales had been falling even though improvements were made from 1898-9 (three forward speeds, a front engine, low-tension magneto ignition, pneumatic tyres, etc.). At the end of 1902 Marius Barbarou, until then Adolphe Clément's works manager (82), was called in with a team of French workmen to redesign the Benz for the modern age. The result was the 'Parsifal' range of 1903, two of which are illustrated. The third new model was the two-cylinder 12/14 h.p. For the first time, Mannheim were offering cars with vertical engines and shaft drive. Later ones had mechanically-operated inlet valves. The engine of the original 8/10 h.p. turned at up to 800 r.p.m., and gave a top road speed of nearly 30 m.p.h. The 16/20-h.p. engine was capable of up to 1000 r.p.m. and drove the car at around 44 m.p.h. The name 'Parsifal' seems to have been kept for the 1904 cars, which included a 16/20 with either shaft or chain drive, and a big 35/40-h.p. chain-driven machine, but by then Barbarou had returned to France, to work for Delaunay-Belleville. Before he went, he had also designed a 60-h.p. racing car, which could reach 75 m.p.h. but was not very successful.

94 GARDNER-SERPOLLET, 1904, France

Between 1889 and 1891, Léon Serpollet designed and had built in Armand

Peugeot's cycle factory around a dozen three-wheeled steamers that were most advanced and effective for their day, in comparison with the infant gasoline automobile, thanks to the Serpollet 'flash' generator (7). When Peugeot turned to gasoline (9), Serpollet occupied himself for the next seven years with steam-powered railcars and trams. During this period, he worked on oil (kerosene) firing instead of coke, devising a dual hand pump which fed water to the generator and oil to the burner simultaneously in constant proportions. Serpollet reverted to the efficient, light personal steam carriage which he had pioneered in 1899, when he obtained backing from the American Frank Gardner. The first of the new series of cars was a 5 h.p. with four cylinders and poppet instead of the slide valves normal with steam engines. The cylinders were disposed vertically at first, and then in transverse, horizontally opposed formation. In 1900 5-, 8-, and 10-h.p. models were marketed. Three years later the water-tank was moved to the front, to provide the appearance of a hood, as was fashionable. The three new models of 1904 included the 18 h.p. illustrated and a 40 h.p., both with donkey-engine operation of the water and oil feed, and a front engine. What appears to be a 'radiator' is in fact the condenser. The silence and smoothness of these cars was fantastic, when compared with gasoline-engined machinery of the day, but they were too expensive and complex even for the steam enthusiast. Not even the 9 h.p., a relatively cheap and simple model with pressure feed, made much impression. Léon Serpollet died in 1907, and his vehicles died with him.

95 NAPIER, 1904,
Great Britain

What was to be the world's first series-production six-cylinder car emerged from the London works of D. Napier & Son late in 1903, in prototype form. The engine, apart from having six cylinders (previously seen only in experimental cars or in vehicles built in desultory fashion), was quite advanced in having overhead inlet valves, mechanically operated. It was claimed to develop 30 b.h.p., at a normal speed of 900 r.p.m. With the flexibility and smoothness derived from six cylinders, only three forward speeds were thought necessary. It was a noisy engine with the severe period of crankshaft vibration common to most early six-cylinder units, but with 4–50 m.p.h. available in top gear, these defects were passed over at first. The cylinders were cast in three pairs. Chassis weight was reasonable, at 17 cwt. Using his own win in the 1902 Gordon Bennett Race and the *réclame* of the new model as weapons, Selwyn Francis Edge, who publicized and sold the Napier, turned it into Britain's best known and most exciting car with his skilful promotion.

96 ROYCE, 1904,
Great Britain

Henry Royce, an engineer with training in the locomotive world, was head of F. H. Royce & Company, manufacturers of electric cranes and dynamos since 1889. His entry into automobile manufacture took a characteristic form. Like other industrialists at the turn of the century, he knew nothing about cars, and like most of them, he could only copy what seemed a good existing design: at this time, original car designers were few indeed, so most employers had to do without them. In any case, Royce was a craftsman-mechanic himself, by aptitude and inclination, not a designer. Most car makers were not even this; they were businessmen only. Because Royce had his special skills, his cars were to be noted for their extremely fine workmanship, which gave rise to their exceptional running qualities. Typically, he took a French car as a guide; France in 1903 was the leader in the automobile world. The 10-h.p. Decauville of that year with which he experimented provided recognizable inspiration; so much so that Royce's car was easily mistaken for one, and imported parts were used, but it was greatly improved upon. For example, the first Royce car, which was running early in 1904, had mechanically-operated overhead inlet valves instead of the Decauville's automatic inlets, and the latter was as untidy under the hood as the little Royce was tidy. Because it was so well made, the Royce was very much quieter and smoother. The engine turned at 1000 r.p.m., providing 12 b.h.p. and 30 m.p.h. Three cars of this type were built. One went to Henry Edmunds, a director of a firm importing continental cars of which the Hon. C. S. Rolls and Claude Johnson were also members. Rolls tried the car, and was so impressed that he undertook to sell Royce's whole output. During 1904 the name Rolls-Royce was used for the first time, applied to an improvement on the original Royce that pioneered

the new familiar radiator form. Although the twin was offered in 1905 and 1906, four- and six-cylinder engines were on show at the Paris Salon late in 1904. A famous partnership had begun.

97 VAUXHALL, 1903, 1904, Great Britain

In one sense it is not inappropriate that General Motors should have owned Vauxhall since 1925, because the Luton firm started life with a small car that was in most respects on the lines of the contemporary 'gas-buggy' typical of the transatlantic scene. The Vauxhall Ironworks of Lambeth, London, were founded by Alex Wilson in 1857 to make marine steam engines. Gasoline engines were added in 1896. From 1897 experimental cars were designed by F. W. Hodges, and in 1903 the firm decided to take a gamble, like so many of their contemporaries, on the new form of transportation. The little 5-h.p. two-passenger machine was intended as an economy runabout. It weighed only $5\frac{1}{2}$ cwt. complete. It was cheap, and starting late in 1903, forty-three were built. This first Vauxhall differed from most of its type in its chassis and suspension: there was integral construction of body and frame, and a coil spring to each wheel. In 1904 improvements were effected by adding a reverse gear and (later) a steering wheel, while the cylinder stroke was lengthened. This type was known as the 6 h.p. The car illustrated above is the first, 1903 type. The lower painting is of the 1904 model, still with tiller steering.

John Kemp Starley of Coventry made his name with bicycles; although he did not invent the safety bicycle, the pioneer of the modern machine, he was the first (in 1885) to put it into production in commercial quantities. Its name was the Rover. The Rover Cycle Company followed up with a motor-cycle in 1902, and the first Rover car appeared in 1904 as an attempt to cash in on what seemed to be the 'coming thing'. Its designer was E. W. Lewis, who had worked for Daimler (86). His original car was most ingenious and advanced. The 8-h.p. engine was at first made in unit with the gear-box and rear axle, without a universal joint in the shaft drive; an assembly which also helped support the body. Though the chassis side members were of wood, the body frame consisted of aluminium castings. The rear axle was unsprung. The little car weighed 11 cwt., and could reach 30 m.p.h. Most of the 8-h.p. Rovers built reverted to conventional frames, sprung rear axles, and universally-jointed shafts, and in this form they sold well. A smaller 6 h.p. followed and accompanied the 8 h.p., and Rover 'singles' were listed until 1912.

INDEX

Make	Model	Ref. No. (colour)	Page No. (description)
Panhard-Levassor	1895	13	115
Panhard-Levassor	6/7 h.p.	65	138
Pennington		16	117
Peugeot	1894	9	114
Peugeot	Bébé	67	139
Popp		26	121
Prinetti & Stucchi		34	125
Rambler		75	143
Renault		54	133
Rochet-Schneider	1895	14	116
Roper	Steamer	1	109
Rover		98	153
Royal Enfield	Quad	46	130
Royce		96	151
Scania	1901	59	136
Scania	1903	91	150
Serpollet	3-wlr	7	112
Standard		84	146
Stephens		24	120
Stoewer		29	122
Sunbeam Mabley		48	131
Thomson		17	118
Vabis	1897	20	119
Vallée		21	119
Vauxhall	1903	97	152
Vauxhall	1904	97	152
Vivinus		42	128
Wartburg		81	145
Weber		72	141
Winton		76	143
Wolseley	10 h.p.	73	141

35!